Music for Analysis

*Examples from the Common Practice Period
and the Twentieth Century*

SEVENTH EDITION

Thomas Benjamin
Peabody Conservatory of the Johns Hopkins University

Michael Horvit   Robert Nelson
Moores School of Music, University of Houston

P 516 Hendemith / P 471 Bartok P. 442 / P 434 Milhaud

New York   Oxford
OXFORD UNIVERSITY PRESS
2010

Oxford University Press, Inc., publishes works that further Oxford University's
objective of excellence in research, scholarship, and education.

Oxford New York
Auckland Cape Town Dar es Salaam Hong Kong Karachi
Kuala Lumpur Madrid Melbourne Mexico City Nairobi
New Delhi Shanghai Taipei Toronto

With offices in
Argentina Austria Brazil Chile Czech Republic France Greece
Guatemala Hungary Italy Japan Poland Portugal Singapore
South Korea Switzerland Thailand Turkey Ukraine Vietnam

Copyright © 2007, 2010 by Oxford University Press, Inc.

© 2001 by Schirmer Thomson Learning

© 1992, 1996 by Wadsworth Publishing Co., Inc.

© 1978, 1984 by Houghton Mifflin Company

Published by Oxford University Press, Inc.
198 Madison Avenue, New York, New York 10016
http://www.oup.com

ISBN   978-0-19-537983-9 (paper)

9 8 7 6 5 4 3 2

Printed in the United States of America
on acid-free paper

Contents

Preface   xix
Suggestions for Using This Book   xxii

Part I   Diatonic Materials
SUGGESTIONS FOR DISCUSSION

1. Tonic Triad
Questions for Analysis

1. HAYDN, *Sonatina in G major, Hob. XVI: 8*   3
2. CZERNY, *Sonatina, op. 792, no. 8*   3
3. RIMSKY-KORSAKOV, *Le Coq d'Or: Hymn to the Sun*   3
4. BEETHOVEN, *Leonora Overture No. 2, op. 72*   4
5. BEETHOVEN, *Trio, op. 70, no. 2*   4
6. CHOPIN, *Polens Grabgesang, op. 74*   5
7. CHOPIN, *Valse (Posthumous)*   6
8. BEETHOVEN, *Symphony No. 5, op. 67*   6
9. COUPERIN, *Carnival*   7

2. Dominant Triad in Root Position
Questions for Analysis

10. MOZART, *Rondo*   8
11. KUHNAU, *Biblical Sonata No. 1: Victory Dance and Festival*   8
12. BEETHOVEN, *Für Elise*   9
13. SCHUMANN, *Album for the Young, op. 68: Reiterstück*   9
14. WEBER, *Euryanthe, op. 81: Overture*   10
15. BEETHOVEN, *Symphony No. 5, op. 67*   10

3. Dominant Seventh and Ninth in Root Position
Questions for Analysis
Model Analysis

16. WEBER, *German Dance*   12
17. MOZART, *Sonata, K. 332*   12
18. SCHUBERT, *Wiegenlied, op. 98, no. 2*   13
19. VERDI, *Rigoletto, Act I, no. 2*   13
20. HAYDN, *Sonata in E major, Hob. XVI: 13*   14
21. BEETHOVEN, *Symphony No. 4, op. 60*   15
22. WEBER, *Oberon: Overture*   15
23. SCHUBERT, *Ländler*   16
24. SCHUBERT, *Valses Nobles, op. 77*   16
25. MOZART, *Valse*   17

4. Subdominant Triad in Root Position
Questions for Analysis

26. SCHEIDT, *Bergamasca*   18
27. SCHUMANN, *Faschingsschwank aus Wien, op. 26, no. 3: Scherzino*   18
28. CHOPIN, *Mazurka, op. 17, no. 1*   19

29. BEETHOVEN, *Egmont Overture, op. 84*   19
30. VERDI, *Rigoletto, Act I, no. 7*   20
31. SCHUBERT, *Impromptu, op. 90, no. 4, D. 899*   21
32. KERN, *Look for the Silver Lining*   22
33. BEETHOVEN, *Seven Country Dances, no. 7*   23
34. SCHUBERT, *Ländler*   23

5. Cadential Tonic Six-Four Chord

Questions for Analysis

35. SCHUBERT, *Valses Sentimentales, op. 50, no. 18*   24
36. CHOPIN, *Mazurka, op. 24, no. 3*   24
37. DONIZETTI, *Lucia di Lammermoor, Act II, no. 6*   25
38. BEETHOVEN, *Trio, op. 97*   26

6. Tonic, Subdominant, and Dominant Triads in First Inversion

Questions for Analysis
Model Analysis

39. BACH, *Lobt Gott, ihr Christen, allzugleich*   29
40. MOZART, *Bastien und Bastienne, K. 46B, no. 9*   29
41. MOZART, *Sonata, K. 332*   30
42. HAYDN, *Sonata in D major, Hob. XVI:37*   30
43. MOZART, *Abendempfindung, K. 523*   31
44. BEETHOVEN, *Symphony No. 5, op. 67*   31
45. BEETHOVEN, *Fidelio, Act I, no. 9*   32
46. MOZART, *Sonata, K. 570*   32
47. MENDELSSOHN, *Elijah, op. 70, no. 29*   32
48. COUPERIN, *Le Petit Rien*   33
49. DANDRIEU, *Les Fifres*   33

7. Supertonic Triad

Questions for Analysis

50. ANONYMOUS, *Dir, dir, Jehovah, will ich singen*   35
51. SCHUBERT, *Waltz, op. 9, no. 3, D. 365*   35
52. BEETHOVEN, *Six Variations on "Nel cor più non mi sento"*   35
53. MOZART, *Die Zauberflöte, K. 620, Act II, no. 21*   36
54. CHOPIN, *Zwei Leichen*   36
55. BEETHOVEN, *Trio, op. 121A*   36
56. VERDI, *Rigoletto, Act II, no. 14*   38
57. CHOPIN, *Mazurka, op. 33, no. 2*   39
58. HAYDN, *Sonata in E minor, Hob. XVI: 34*   39

8. Inversions of the Dominant Seventh Chord

Questions for Analysis

59. J. C. F. BACH, *Nun danket alle Gott*   40
60. HAYDN, *Sonata in C major, Hob. XVI: 35*   40
61. PAISIELLO, *Le donne sur balcone*   40
62. MOZART, *Quartet, K. 464*   41
63. BEETHOVEN, *Sonata, op. 31, no. 3*   41
64. RAMEAU, *Sarabande I, vol. I*   42
65. HAYDN, *Trio in C major, Hob. XV: 3*   42
66. KUHLAU, *Sonatina, op. 20, no. 1*   43
67. BEETHOVEN, *Symphony No. 2, op. 36*   44
68. BEETHOVEN, *Minuet in C*   44

9. Linear (Embellishing) Six-Four Chords
Questions for Analysis

69. BEETHOVEN, *Concerto No. 1 for Piano, op. 15*   45
70. SCHUBERT, *Valses Sentimentales, op. 50, no. 1, D. 779*   45
71. MOZART, *Rondo, K. 485*   46
72. HAYDN, *Quartet, op. 3, no. 5*   47
73. SCHUBERT, *Waltz, op. 9, no. 1, D. 365*   47
74. KUHLAU, *Sonatina, op. 88, no. 3*   48
75. MOZART, *Symphony No. 35, K. 385*   48
76. BEETHOVEN, *Sonatina in G major*   49
77. BEETHOVEN, *Symphony No. 7, op. 92*   49
78. MOZART, *Symphony No. 41, K. 551*   51
79. HAYDN, *Sonata in D major, Hob. XVI: 37*   51
80. BEETHOVEN, *Contradanse*   52
81. BUXTEHUDE, *Passacaglia*   52
82. BEETHOVEN, *Symphony No. 3, op. 55*   53
83. GOUNOD, *Faust, Act I, no. 6*   53
84. SULLIVAN, *H.M.S. Pinafore, "I'm Called Little Buttercup"*   55

10. Submediant and Mediant Triads
Questions for Analysis

85. CRÜGER, *Herzliebster Jesu, was hast du verbrochen*   56
86. ANONYMOUS, *Dir, dir, Jehovah, will ich singen*   56
87. BACH, *Schmücke dich, o liebe Seele*   56
88. MOZART, *Bastien und Bastienne, K. 46B, no. 1*   57
89. MOZART, *Sonata, K. 545*   57
90. HANDEL, *Sonata in F for Flute and Continuo*   58
91. VERDI, *Rigoletto, Act I, no. 1*   58
92. BRAHMS, *Symphony No. 4, op. 98*   58
93. CORELLI, *Sonata for Violin and Continuo, op. 5, no. 9*   59
94. SCHUBERT, *Quartet in D major, D. 74*   59
95. BEETHOVEN, *Trio, op. 1, no. 3*   60
96. MOZART, *Sonata, K. 283*   61
97. J. C. F. BACH, *Menuet*   61
98. TESSIER, *Au joli bois je m'en vais*   62
99. STRAUSS, *Der Rosenkavalier, Act III*   62
100. BRAHMS, *Romance, op. 118, no. 5*   63
101. SCHUMANN, *Phantasiestücke, op. 12, no. 4, Grillen*   64
102. SCHUBERT, *Im Abendroth (Posthumous)*   64
103. SCHUBERT, *Symphony in C major ("The Great")*   65

11. Leading Tone Triad
Questions for Analysis

104. TESCHNER, *Schatz über alle Schätze*   67
105. BACH, *Aus meines Herzens Grunde*   67
106. SCHUMANN, *Album for the Young, op. 68: Soldatenmarsch*   67
107. HANDEL, *Courante*   67
108. HAYDN, *Sonata in E♭ major, Hob. XVI: 49*   68
109. HAYDN, *Sonatina in D major, Hob. XVI: 4*   68
110. MOZART, *Sonata, K. 280*   69
111. DAQUIN, *La Joyeuse*   70

12. Variant Qualities of Diatonic Triads
Questions for Analysis

SCALAR VARIANTS IN MINOR

112.	BACH, *Herr, ich habe mißgehandelt*	71
113.	PACHELBEL, *Chaconne*	71
114.	TELEMANN, *Fantasie No. 8*	71
115.	BYRD, *Pavana "The Earle of Salisbury"*	72
116.	A. SCARLATTI, *Folia* ⊙	72
117.	MATTHESON, *Minuet* ⊙	73
118.	MOZART, *Sonata, K. 310* ⊙	73

MODAL BORROWING

119.	VERDI, *La Traviata, Act I, no. 4*	74
120.	DONIZETTI, *Linda di Chamounix, "O luce di quest'anima"*	75
121.	MOZART, *Sonata for Violin and Piano, K. 306*	76
122.	HAYDN, *Sonatina in C major, Hob. XVI: 7* ⊙	77
123.	SCHUBERT, *Aufenthalt*	77
124.	SCHUBERT, *Der Wanderer*	78
125.	BRAHMS, *Symphony No. 3, op. 90*	79
126.	VERDI, *Il Trovatore, Act II, no. 11*	80
127.	BEETHOVEN, *Symphony No. 5, op. 67*	81
128.	BRAHMS, *Symphony No. 4, op. 98*	82

13. Supertonic Seventh Chord
Questions for Analysis

129.	ANONYMOUS, *Herr, wie du willst, so schick's mit mir* ⊙	83
130.	BACH, *Straf' mich nicht in deinem Zorn*	83
131.	HAYDN, *Sonata in A♭ major, Hob. XVI: 46*	83
132.	GRIEG, *Voegtersang* ⊙	84
133.	BEETHOVEN, *Symphony No. 6, op. 68*	84
134.	SCHUBERT, *Quartet, op. 168, D. 112*	85
135.	MOZART, *Sonata, K. 310* ⊙	85
136.	SCHUBERT, *Ständchen*	86
137.	BEETHOVEN, *Symphony No. 2, op. 36*	87
138.	BEETHOVEN, *Sonata, op. 14, no. 2* ⊙	87
139.	BEETHOVEN, *Symphony No. 6, op. 68*	88
140.	BIZET, *Carmen, Act II: Entr'acte*	89
141.	RODGERS, *Blue Moon*	89

14. Leading Tone Seventh Chord
Questions for Analysis

142.	DVORAK, *Quartet, op. 96*	91
143.	MOZART, *Sonata, K. 457* ⊙	91
144.	SCHUMANN, *Carnaval, op. 9: Chiarina* ⊙	91
145.	BRAHMS, *Ballade, op. 10, no. 4* ⊙	92
146.	HANDEL, *Sonata for Flute and Continuo*	92
147.	HAYDN (?), *Allegro* ⊙	93
148.	HAYDN, *Trio in G major, Hob. XV: 25*	93
149.	MOZART, *Requiem, K. 626: Offertorium*	94
150.	HAYDN, *Sonatina in G major, Hob. XVI: 11* ⊙	95
151.	HANDEL, *Judas Maccabaeus, Part III: no. 53, Introduction*	96
152.	WAGNER, *Das Rheinghold, Scene 1*	97
153.	GLUCK, *Orphée, Act I, no. 1*	99
154.	HANDEL, *Aria con Variazioni, Leçon No. 1*	100

155. TELEMANN, *Fantasia, 1er Dozzina, no. 5*   101
156. MOZART, *Sonata for Violin and Piano, K. 306*   101

15. Other Diatonic Seventh Chords
Questions for Analysis

157. BACH, *O Ewigkeit, du Donnerwort*   103
158. MOZART, *Rondo. K. 494*   103
159. MENDELSSOHN, *Kinderstück, op. 72, no. 1*   103
160. PACHELBEL, *Fantasie*   104
161. HANDEL, *Sonata for Flute and Continuo*   104
162. HANDEL, *Leçon No. 2, Menuet*   105
163. TCHAIKOVSKY, *Symphony No. 4, op. 36*   105
164. BACH, *French Suite in D minor*   105

16. Complete Pieces for Analysis I
Checklist for Analysis

165. BEETHOVEN, *Minuet*   107
166. SCHUBERT, *Dance*   108
167. SCHUBERT, *German Dance, op. 33, no. 12*   108
168. BEETHOVEN, *Scottish Dance*   109
169. PURCELL, *Rigadoon*   110
170. RAMEAU, *Minuet*   111
171. WITT, *Passacaglia*   112
172. GRIEG, *Norsk*   114

Part II Chromatic Materials
SUGGESTIONS FOR DISCUSSION

17. Secondary (Applied, Borrowed) Dominants
Questions for Analysis
Model Analysis

173. BEETHOVEN, *Trio, op. 1, no. 1*   120
174. MOZART, *Sonata, K. 281*   120
175. SCHUBERT, *Impromptu, op. 142, no. 3*   121
176. HAYDN, *Trio in D major*   121
177. BEETHOVEN, *Sonatina in G major*   122
178. WEBER, *Oberon: Overture*   122
179. BEETHOVEN, *Trio, op. 1, no. 1*   123
180. SCHUMANN, *Sonata, op. 118ᶜ, Andante*   124
181. BEETHOVEN, *Symphony No. 1, op. 21*   124
182. HANDEL, *Suite XI*   125
183. SCHUMANN, *Arabeske, op. 18*   125
184. BEETHOVEN, *Symphony No. 4, op. 60*   126
185. SCHUMANN, *Widmung, op. 25, no. 1*   127
186. SCHUBERT, *Symphony No. 8 ("Unfinished")*   128
187. SCHUMANN, *Sonata, op. 118ᶜ, Puppenwiegenlied*   128
188. SCHUBERT, *Quintet ("Die Forelle"), op. 114, D. 667*   129
189. BEETHOVEN, *Quintet, op. 29*   130
190. BEETHOVEN, *Trio, op. 11*   131
191. VERDI, *Rigoletto, Act II, no. 7*   132
192. HANDEL, *Suite XVI*   134
193. BEETHOVEN, *Sonata, op. 53*   134
194. SCHUBERT, *Symphony in C major ("The Great")*   134

195. BEETHOVEN, *Trio, op. 1, no. 3*   135
196. SCHUBERT, *Mass in E♭ major: Benedictus*   136
197. MENDELSSOHN, *Midsummer Night's Dream, op. 61: Wedding March*   137
198. VERDI, *Rigoletto, Act II, no. 14*   138
199. BACH, *Christmas Oratorio, no. 4: Introduction*   138
200. HANDEL, *Sonata VII for Flute and Continuo*   139
201. CHOPIN, *Mazurka, op. 67, no. 2*   140
202. CHOPIN, *Valse, op. 69, no. 1*   140
203. CHOPIN, *Valse Brillante, op. 34, no. 3*   141
204. GERSHWIN, *Someone to Watch Over Me*   142
205. TCHAIKOVSKY, *Morning Prayer*   143

18. Modulation to Closely Related Keys
Questions for Analysis
MODULATION TO DOMINANT

206. MOZART, *Symphony No. 39, K. 543*   144
207. MOZART, *Sonata, K. 331*   144
208. BEETHOVEN, *Symphony No. 2, op. 36*   145
209. HAYDN, *Minuet*   145
210. SCHUBERT, *Quartet, D. 173*   146
211. HAYDN, *Sonata in C♯ minor, Hob. XVI: 36*   146
212. MOZART, *Symphony No. 41, K. 551*   147
213. CHOPIN, *Mazurka, op. 7, no. 2*   148
214. HAYDN, *Sonata in G major, Hob. XVI: 39*   148
215. MOZART, *Sonata, K. 282, Menuet I*   149
216. SCHUBERT, *Quartet, D. 173*   150

MODULATION TO RELATIVE MAJOR

217. HAYDN, *Trio in F♯ minor, Hob. XV: 26*   152
218. HAYDN, *Sonata in E minor, Hob. XVI: 34*   153
219. MOZART, *Sonata, K. 330*   153
220. DONIZETTI, *Lucia di Lammermoor, Act I, Cavatina*   154
221. BRAHMS, *Quintet, op. 115*   155
222. BEETHOVEN, *Symphony No. 7, op. 92*   156
223. HAYDN, *Symphony No. 104, Hob. I: 104*   156

MODULATION TO OTHER CLOSELY RELATED KEYS

224. HAYDN, *Sonatina, Hob. XVI: 1*   158
225. BONONCINI, *Deh più a me non vàscondete*   158
226. SAINT-SAËNS, *Carneval des Animaux: Le Cygne*   159
227. BRAHMS, *Waltz, op. 39, no. 15*   161
228. BEETHOVEN, *Quartet, op. 18, no. 2*   161
229. PURCELL, *Dido and Aeneas, Act I, scene I*   162
230. BACH, *French Suite in C Minor*   163

19. Complete Pieces for Analysis II
Checklist for Analysis

231. BACH, *Wachet auf, ruft uns die Stimme*   164
232. BACH, *In dulci jubilo*   165
233. BACH, *Christ lag in Todesbanden*   166
234. HANDEL, *Menuet*   167
235. BEETHOVEN, *Sonata, op. 26*   168
236. SCHUMANN, *Sonata, op. 118ᵇ, Abendlied*   169

237. BRAHMS, *Waltz, op. 39*   170
238. HANDEL, *Prelude*   171
239. BEETHOVEN, *Sonatina in F major*   172
240. HAYDN, *Sonata in G major, Hob. XVI: 27*   174
241. GERSHWIN, *I Got Rhythm*   178

20. Linear (Embellishing) Diminished Seventh Chords

Questions for Analysis

242. HAYDN, *Symphony No. 104, Hob. I: 104, Menuet*   180
243. BEETHOVEN, *Symphony No. 7, op. 92*   180
244. LISZT, *Les Préludes*   181
245. BEETHOVEN, *Contradanse*   182
246. TCHAIKOVSKY, *Symphony No. 6, op. 74*   182
247. BEETHOVEN, *Quartet, op. 18, no. 3*   183
248. SCHUBERT, *Sonata, op. 53*   183
249. GOUNOD, *Faust, Act IV, no. 18*   184
250. SCHUMANN, *Carnaval, op. 9: Arlequin*   185
251. MOZART, *Waltz, K. 567*   185
252. WAGNER, *Rienzi: Overture*   186
253. BELLINI, *I Puritani, Act II, scene 3*   186
254. HAYDN, *Symphony No. 104, Hob. I: 104*   187
255. RODGERS, *The Girl Friend*   188
256. BRAHMS, *Liebeslieder Walzer, op. 52, no. 4*   190

21. Neapolitan Triad

Questions for Analysis

257. MOZART, *Concerto in A major, K. 488*   192
258. SCHUBERT, *Der Müller und der Bach*   192
259. BACH, *Ach Gott, vom Himmel sieh' darein*   194
260. BACH, *Invention No. 13*   194
261. VERDI, *Il Trovatore, Act II, no. 8*   195
262. BRAHMS, *Intermezzo in A major, op. 118, no. 2*   196
263. CHOPIN, *Prelude, op. 28, no. 20*   197
264. BEETHOVEN, *String Quartet, op. 59, no. 2*   198
265. BRAHMS, *Wie Melodien zieht es mir, op. 105*   199
266. BEETHOVEN, *Quartet, op. 18, no. 3*   199
267. SCHUBERT, *Mass in E♭ major: Credo*   200
268. BACH, *The Well-Tempered Clavier, Vol. II, Fugue 17*   201
269. CHOPIN, *Prelude, op. 28, no. 6*   202

22. Augmented Sixth Chords, Submediant Degree as Lowest Note

Questions for Analysis
Model Analysis

ITALIAN

270. BACH, *Ich hab' mein' Sach' Gott heimgestellt*   205
271. BEETHOVEN, *Bagatelle, op. 119, no. 1*   205
272. BEETHOVEN, *Coriolan Overture, op. 62*   205
273. TCHAIKOVSKY, *Mazurka*   206
274. SCHUBERT, *Quartet, op. 168, D. 112*   206
275. BEETHOVEN, *Symphony No. 1, op. 21*   207

GERMAN

276. MOZART, *Sonata, K. 457* · 208
277. BEETHOVEN, *Sonata, op. 109* · · · · · · · · · · · · · · · · · 209
278. HAYDN, *Trio, Hob. XV: 25* · 209
279. BEETHOVEN, *Thirty-Two Variations, Var. 30* · · · · · · 210
280. SIBELIUS, *Chanson Sans Paroles, op. 40, no. 2* · · · · · 210
281. STRAUSS, *Der Rosenkavalier, Act I* · · · · · · · · · · · · · · 211

FRENCH

282. MENDELSSOHN, *Elijah, op. 70, no. 1* · · · · · · · · · · · · 212
283. SCHUBERT, *Mass in G major: Kyrie* · · · · · · · · · · · · · 213
284. BACH, *Wer nur den lieben Gott läßt walten* · · · · · · · · 214
285. SCHUBERT, *Sonata, op. 42* · · · · · · · · · · · · · · · · · · · 214
286. VERDI, *La Traviata, Act III: Prelude* · · · · · · · · · · · · 215
287. SCHUBERT, *Symphony in C major ("The Great")* · · · · 215
288. GRIEG, *Alfedans, op. 12* · 216
289. HERBERT, *Gypsy Love Song* · · · · · · · · · · · · · · · · · · · 217

ENHARMONIC GERMAN

290. SCHUMANN, *Dichterliebe, op. 48, no. 12: "Am leuchtenden Sommermorgen"* · 218

23. Augmented Sixth Chords, Other Scale Degrees as Lowest Note
Questions for Analysis

291. MOZART (?), *Adagio* · 220
292. GRANADOS, *Valses Poeticos* · · · · · · · · · · · · · · · · · · 220
293. SCHUBERT, *Symphony No. 8 ("Unfinished")* · · · · · · · 221
294. MOUSSORGSKY, *Songs and Dances of Death, no. 4* · · 222
295. GLUCK, *Orphée, Act I, nos. 6 and 7* · · · · · · · · · · · · · 223

24. Augmented Sixth Chords, Other Uses
Question for Analysis

LINEAR

296. VERDI, *Rigoletto, Act I: Prelude* · · · · · · · · · · · · · · · · 224
297. TCHAIKOVSKY, *Song Without Words* · · · · · · · · · · · · 224
298. TCHAIKOVSKY, *Romeo and Juliet* · · · · · · · · · · · · · · · 225
299. SCHUBERT, *Waltz* · 226
300. BRAHMS, *Intermezzo, op. 76, no. 4* · · · · · · · · · · · · · 226
301. TCHAIKOVSKY, *The Witch* · 227

SECONDARY

302. CHOPIN, *Prelude, op. 28, no. 22* · · · · · · · · · · · · · · · 228
303. SCHUBERT, *Mass in G major: Benedictus* · · · · · · · · · 228
304. SCHUBERT, *Die Allmacht, op. 79, no. 2* · · · · · · · · · · 230

ALTERED DOMINANTS

305. SCHUBERT, *Quintet, op. 163* · · · · · · · · · · · · · · · · · · 231
306. LISZT, *Liebestraum, no. 3* · 232
307. RIMSKY-KORSAKOV, *Snowmaiden, Chanson du Bonhomme Hiver* · 232
308. GRIEG, *Solvejg's Lied* · 233

25. Other Means of Modulation

Question for Analysis
Model Analysis

309. SCHUBERT, *Mass in G major: Gloria*   235
310. BRAHMS, *Wenn du nur zuweilen lächelst, op. 57, no. 2*   236
311. BEETHOVEN, *Symphony No. 5, op. 67*   237
312. SCHUBERT, *Waltz, op. 9, no. 14, D. 365*   238
313. MOZART, *Die Entführung aus dem Serail, K. 384, Act III, no. 18*   238
314. SCHUMANN, *Symphony No. 2, op. 61*   240
315. BEETHOVEN, *Symphony No. 7, op. 92*   240
316. HAYDN, *String Quartet, op. 76, no. 6*   241
317. BEETHOVEN, *Sonata, op. 13*   242
318. BEETHOVEN, *Trio, op. 70, no. 1*   243
319. SCRIABIN, *Prelude, op. 13, no. 3*   244
320. J. STRAUSS, *Die Fledermaus: Overture*   245
321. BRAHMS, *Wie bist du meine Königen, op. 32, no. 9*   245
322. SCHUBERT, *Mass in A♭ major: Agnus Dei*   247
323. BEETHOVEN, *Trio, op. 11*   249
324. RACHMANINOFF, *Melodie, op. 3, no. 3*   251
325. SCHUBERT, *Symphony No. 8 ("Unfinished")*   252

26. Ninth Chords

Questions for Analysis

DOMINANT NINTHS

326. J. STRAUSS, *Artist's Life Waltzes, op. 316, no. 3*   253
327. FRANCK, *Sonata for Violin and Piano*   253
328. BEETHOVEN, *Theme from Six Easy Variations*   254
329. CHOPIN, *Valse Brillante, op. 34, no. 1*   255
330. SCHUMANN, *Waldesgespräch, op. 39, no. 3*   255
331. CHOPIN, *Prelude, op. 28, no. 15*   256

SECONDARY DOMINANT NINTHS

332. BACH, *St. Matthew Passion, no. 78*   258
333. SCHUMANN, *Genoveva, op. 81: Overture*   258
334. GRIEG, *Grandmother's Minuet, op. 68, no. 2*   260
335. SCHUMANN, *Kinderszenen, op. 15, no. 7: Träumerei*   260

NONDOMINANT NINTHS

336. GRIEG, *Wedding Day at Troldhaugen, op. 65, no. 6*   261
337. MENDELSSOHN, *Midsummer Night's Dream, op. 21: Overture*   262
338. FAURÉ, *Après un Rêve*   262

27. Extended Linear Usages

Questions for Analysis
Model Analysis

339. CHOPIN, *Mazurka, op. 6, no. 1*   265
340. BRAHMS, *"Der Tod, das ist die kühle Nacht," op. 96, no. 1*   266
341. WEBER, *Euryanthe: Overture*   267
342. BRAHMS, *Variations on a Theme by Handel, var. 20*   267
343. FRANCK, *Symphony in D minor*   268
344. WAGNER, *Lohengrin, Act I, scene 2*   269
345. WAGNER, *Wotan's Farewell, Die Walküre, Act III*   270
346. CHOPIN, *Prelude, op. 28, no. 9*   272
347. BEETHOVEN, *Quartet, op. 18, no. 6*   273

28. Complete Pieces for Analysis III
Checklist for Analysis

348.	BACH, *Ein' feste Burg ist unser Gott*	276
349.	BACH, *Es ist genug, so nimm, Herr*	277
350.	MOZART, *Minuet, K. 355*	278
351.	SCHUMANN, *Myrthen, op. 25, no. 24*	281
352.	MENDELSSOHN, *Lieder ohne Wörte, op. 30, no. 3*	282
353.	CHOPIN, *Mazurka, Op. posth. 67, no. 2*	284
354.	SCHUMANN, *Phantasiestücke, op. 12, no. 3: Warum?*	286
355.	GRIEG, *Erotikon*	288
356.	LISZT, *Il pensieroso, from Années de Pèlerinage*	290
357.	R. STRAUSS, *Morgen, op. 27, no. 4*	292
358.	WAGNER, *Der Engel*	295
359.	BEETHOVEN, *Sieben Variationen über das Volkslied: "God Save the King"*	299
360.	MOZART, *Symphony No. 40, K. 550*	305
361.	BEACH, *Phantoms*	310
362.	JOPLIN, *A Breeze from Alabama: March and Two-Step*	315
363.	WAGNER, *Prelude Act I Tristan und Isolde*	317
364.	MOZART, *Sonata, K. 309*	324
	I. *Allegro con spirito*	324
	II. *Andante, un poco Adagio*	329
	III. *Allegretto grazioso*	333
365.	BEETHOVEN, *Sonata, op. 2, no. 3*	343
	I. *Allegro con brio*	343
	II. *Adagio*	355
	III. *Scherzo, Allegro*	360
	IV. *Allegro assai*	364

29. Examples of Counterpoint
Questions for Analysis

366.	BACH, *Cantata No. 4: Sinfonia*	375
367.	BACH, *Chorale Prelude on "In Dulci Jubilo"*	376
368.	BACH, *Chorale Prelude on "Christ lag in Todesbanden"*	379
369.	BRAHMS, *Chorale Prelude on "O Wie selig seid ihr doch, ihr Frommen"*	380
370.	PURCELL, *"Thy hand Belinda", from Dido and Aeneas*	382
371.	BACH, *Invention No. 4, BWV 775*	386
372.	BACH, *Invention No. 13, BWV 775*	388
373.	BACH, *Sinfonia 3, BWV 789*	389
374.	BACH, *The Well-Tempered Clavier, Vol. I, Fugue 2*	391
375.	BACH, *The Well-Tempered Clavier, Vol. II, Fugue 9*	394
376.	MENDELSSOHN, *Fugue No. 2, op. 35*	397

Additional Examples for the Study
of Contrapuntual Techniques

Part III   Contemporary Materials
SUGGESTIONS FOR DISCUSSION
Model Analysis

30. Extended and Altered Tertian Harmony
Questions for Analysis

377.	HANSON, *Symphony No. 2, op. 30*	405
378.	KABALEVSKY, *Sonatina, op. 13*	405

379. HOVHANESS, *Mysterious Mountain*	406
380. SHOSTAKOVICH, *Prelude, op. 34, no. 24*	407
381. DEBUSSY, *Pelléas et Méllisande, Act I, scene 1*	407
382. SCRIABIN, *Poem, op. 32, no. 2*	408
383. RAVEL, *Valses Nobles et Sentimentales*	409
384. RODGERS, *Slaughter on Tenth Avenue*	410
385. ELLINGTON, *Prelude to a Kiss*	411
386. DUKE JORDAN, *Jordu*	412
387. BERG, *Four Songs, op. 2, no. 3*	413
388. RAKSIN, *Laura*	415

31. Diatonic (Church) Modes
Questions for Analysis
Model Analysis

389. BARTÓK, *Little Pieces for Children, no. III*	421
390. CHÁVEZ, *Ten Preludes, no. 1*	422
391. POULENC, *Valse*	422
392. DEBUSSY, *Trois Chansons, no. 1*	424
393. KABALEVSKY, *Toccatina*	424
394. BRITTEN, *Ceremony of Carols, no. 8*	425
395. DEBUSSY, *Suite bergamasque, Passepied*	427
396. FLOYD, *Susannah, Act II, scene 3*	427
397. STRAVINSKY, *Five Fingers: Lento*	428
398. BARTÓK, *Fourteen Bagatelles, op. 6, no. 4*	429
399. CASELLA, *Siciliana*	430
400. ADDERLEY, *Work Song*	432

32. Pandiatonicism and Additive Harmony
Questions for Analysis

401. RAVEL, *Mother Goose Suite: The Magic Garden*	433
402. MILHAUD, *Touches Blanches*	434
403. COWELL, *The Irishman Dances*	434
404. COPLAND, *The Young Pioneers*	435
405. BARBER, *Excursions, III*	435
406. STRAVINSKY, *Petroushka, Danse Russe*	436
407. POULENC, *Gloria, Laudamus te*	437

33. Exotic (Artificial, Synthetic) Scales
Questions for Analysis

408. MILHAUD, *Touches Noires*	438
409. BARTÓK, *Mikrokosmos, no. 78: Five Tone Scale*	438
410. KODÁLY, *Valsette*	439
411. VAUGHAN WILLIAMS, *London Symphony*	440
412. DEBUSSY, *Préludes, II: Voiles*	440
413. BARTÓK, *Mikrokosmos, no. 136: Whole Tone Scale*	441
414. DEBUSSY, *Pelléas et Mélisande, Act II, scene 1*	441
415. BARTÓK, *Fourteen Bagatelles, op. 6, no. 10*	442
416. LUTOSLAWSKI, *Bucolic, no. 3*	442
417. BARTÓK, *Mikrokosmos, no. 101: Diminished Fifth*	443
418. BARTÓK, *Sketches, op. 9, no. 6*	444
419. BARTÓK, *Fourteen Bagatelles, op. 6, no. 6*	446

34. Quartal and Secundal Harmony
Questions for Analysis

420.	HINDEMITH, *Mathis der Maler: Grablegung*	447
421.	IVES, *Majority*	447
422.	KRENEK, *Piano Piece, op. 39, no. 5*	448
423.	HINDEMITH, *Ludus Tonalis, Fuga secunda in G*	449
424.	BARTÓK, *Concerto for Orchestra*	449
425.	BERG, *Wozzeck, Act II*	451
426.	BARTÓK, *Mikrokosmos, no. 107: Melody in the Mist*	452
427.	BERG, *Wozzeck, Act II*	453
428.	COWELL, *Tiger*	454
429.	IVES, *Majority*	455
430.	BRUBECK, *Blue Rondo à la Turk*	456

35. Polyharmony and Polytonality
Questions for Analysis

431.	HONEGGER, *Symphony No. 5*	458
432.	SCHUMAN, *A Three-Score Set, II*	458
433.	KRAFT, *Allegro Giocoso*	459
434.	STRAVINSKY, *The Rake's Progress: Prelude*	460
435.	STRAVINSKY, *Petroushka, Scene 2*	461
436.	MILHAUD, *Saudades do Brazil, no 7: Corcovado*	462
437.	BARTÓK, *Forty-Four Violin Duets, no. 33*	462
438.	BRUBECK, *Strange Meadowlark*	463

36. Free Atonality
Questions for Analysis

439.	SCHÖNBERG, *Drei Klavierstücke, op. 11, no. 1*	465
440.	SCHÖNBERG, *Klavierstücke, op. 19, no. 2*	466
441.	SCHÖNBERG, *Pierrot Lunaire, op. 21, no. 1: Mondestrunken*	467
442.	WEBERN, *Five Movements for String Quartet, op. 5, no. 4*	470
443.	BARTÓK, *Mikrokosmos, no. 144: Minor Seconds, Major Sevenths*	471
444.	BARTÓK, *Fourth String Quartet*	472
445.	BERGER, *Two Episodes, I*	474

37. Twelve-Tone Serialism
Questions for Analysis
Model Analysis

446.	KRENEK, *Dancing Toys, op. 83, no. 1*	478
447.	SCHÖNBERG, *Suite für Klavier, op. 25: Gavotte*	480
448.	DALLAPICCOLA, *Cinque Frammenti di Saffo*	481
449.	WEBERN, *Drei Lieder, op. 25, no. 1*	484

38. Music Since 1945
Questions for Analysis

450.	STOCKHAUSEN, *Klavierstücke, no. 2*	486
451.	LUTOSLAWSKI, *String Quartet (1965)*	487
452.	PENDERECKI, *String Quartet, no. 2*	488
453.	CRUMB, *Madrigals, Book IV*	491
454.	DRUCKMAN, *Valentine, for solo contrabass*	492
455.	ROUSE, *Valentine*	493
456.	HORNE, *Six Short Studies, Sixteenth Notes*	494

39. Complete Pieces for Analysis IV
Suggestion for Analysis

457. RAVEL, *Sonatine, Mouv^t II* 496
458. DEBUSSY, *Pour le Piano: Sarabande* 499
459. DEBUSSY, *Préludes, X: La Cathédrale engloutie* 503
460. MILHAUD, Saudades do Brazil, No. 6: Gavea 508
461. PROKOFIEV, *Classical Symphony, op. 25* 511
462. PROKOFIEV, *March from The Love of Three Oranges* 513
463. HINDEMITH, *Ludus Tonalis, Fuga undecima in B (Canon)* 516
464. RUGGLES, *Evocations, no. 1* 518
465. SCHÖNBERG, *Suite für Klavier, op. 25: Menuett* 519
466. PORTER, *Night and Day* 522
467. GERSHWIN, *Porgy and Bess, "Summertime"* 527
468. STRAVINSKY, *Sonata for Two Pianos, II: Theme with Variations* 531
469. HINDEMITH, *Piano Sonata, No. 2* 542
470. MACMILLAN, *Piano Sonata, I* 546

Appendix A. Checklist for Analysis and Sample Analysis 549
Appendix B. For Further Reference 553
Appendix C. Textbook Correlation Chart 554
Acknowledgments 557
Index of Composers and Their Compositions 561
Index of Complete Pieces 569

CD Track List

Track 1.
2. CZERNY, *Sonatina, op. 792, no. 8*
7. CHOPIN, *Valse (Posthumous)* (:06)

Track 2.
10. MOZART, *Rondo*
11. KUHNAU, *Biblical Sonata No. 1: Victory Dance and Festival* (:10)
12. BEETHOVEN, *Für Elise* (:23)

Track 3.
16. WEBER, *German Dance*
17. MOZART, *Sonata, K. 332, III, m. 15* (:09)
20. HAYDN, *Sonata in E major, Hob. XVI: 13* (:22)
23. SCHUBERT, *Ländler* (:30)
24. SCHUBERT, *Valses Nobles, op. 77* (:43)

Track 4.
26. SCHEIDT, *Bergamasca*
27. SCHUMANN, *Faschingsschwank aus Wien, op. 26, no. 3: Scherzino* (:18)
28. CHOPIN, *Mazurka, op. 17, no. 1* (:31)
31. SCHUBERT, *Impromptu, op. 90, no. 4, D. 899* (:47)
33. BEETHOVEN, *Seven Country Dances, no. 7* (1:10)
34. SCHUBERT, *Ländler* (1:31)

Track 5.
35. SCHUBERT, *Valses Sentimentales, op. 50, no. 18*

Track 6.
39. BACH, *Lobt Gott, ihr Christen, allzugleich*
41. MOZART, *Sonata, K. 332, I, m. 145* (:13)
42. HAYDN, *Sonata in D major, Hob. XVI:37, III m. 114* (:24)
46. MOZART, *Sonata, K. 570* (:36)
48. COUPERIN, *Le Petit Rien* (1:03)

Track 7.
50. ANONYMOUS, *Dir, dir, Jehovah, will ich singen*
51. SCHUBERT, *Waltz, op. 9, no. 3, D. 365* (:15)
52. BEETHOVEN, *Six Variations on "Nel cor più non mi sento"* (:26)
57. CHOPIN, *Mazurka, op. 33, no. 2* (:39)

Track 8.
59. J. C. F. BACH, *Nun danket alle Gott*
60. HAYDN, *Sonata in C major, Hob. XVI: 35* (:25)
63. BEETHOVEN, *Sonata, op. 31, no. 3* (:35)
66. KUHLAU, *Sonatina, op. 20, no. 1* (:50)
68. BEETHOVEN, *Minuet in C* (1:01)

Track 9.
70. SCHUBERT, *Valses Sentimentales, op. 50, no. 1, D. 779*
71. MOZART, *Rondo, K. 485* (:12)
73. SCHUBERT, *Waltz, op. 9, no. 1, D. 365* (:39)
74. KUHLAU, *Sonatina, op. 88, no. 3* (:48)
76. BEETHOVEN, *Sonatina in G major* (1:00)
79. HAYDN, *Sonata in D major, Hob. XVI: 37* (1:18)
80. BEETHOVEN, *Contradanse* (1:35)

Track 10.
85. CRÜGER, *Herzliebster Jesu, was hast du verbrochen*
86. ANONYMOUS, *Dir, dir, Jehovah, will ich singen* (:22)
87. BACH, *Schmücke dich, o liebe Seele* (:44)
89. MOZART, *Sonata, K. 545* (1:14)
96. MOZART, *Sonata, K. 283* (1:24)
97. J. C. F. BACH, *Menuet* (1:42)
100. BRAHMS, *Romance, op. 118, no. 5* (2:03)
101. SCHUMANN, *Phantasiestücke, op. 12, no. 4, Grillen* (2:24)

Track 11.
105. BACH, *Aus meines Herzens Grunde*
106. SCHUMANN, *Album for the Young, op. 68: Soldatenmarsch* (:25)
108. HAYDN, *Sonata in E♭ major, Hob. XVI: 49* (:33)
109. HAYDN, *Sonatina in D major, Hob. XVI: 4* (:45)
110. MOZART, *Sonata, K. 280* (:58)

Track 12.
116. A. SCARLATTI, *Folia*
117. MATTHESON, *Minuet* (:18)
118. MOZART, *Sonata, K. 310* (:28)
122. HAYDN, *Sonatina in C major, Hob. XVI: 7* (:34)

Track 13.
129. ANONYMOUS, *Herr, wie du willst, so schick's mit mir*
132. GRIEG, *Voegtersang* (:29)
135. MOZART, *Sonata, K. 310* (:51)
138. BEETHOVEN, *Sonata, op. 14, no. 2* (1:03)

Track 14.
143. MOZART, *Sonata, K. 457*

Track 15.
144. SCHUMANN, *Carnaval, op. 9: Chiarina*

Track 16.
145. BRAHMS, *Ballade, op. 10, no. 4*

Track 17.
147. HAYDN (?), *Allegro*

Track 18.
150. HAYDN, *Sonatina in G major, Hob. XVI: 11*

Track 19.
157. BACH, *O Ewigkeit, du Donnerwort*

Track 20.
159. MENDELSSOHN, *Kinderstück, op. 72, no. 1*

Track 21.
164. BACH, *French Suite in D minor*

Track 22.
165. BEETHOVEN, *Minuet*

Track 23.
166. SCHUBERT, *Dance*

Track 24.
167. SCHUBERT, *German Dance, op. 33, no. 12*

Track 25.
168. BEETHOVEN, *Scottish Dance*

Track 26.
171. WITT, *Passacaglia*

Track 27.
174. MOZART, *Sonata, K. 281*

Track 28.
175. SCHUBERT, *Impromptu, op. 142, no. 3*

Track 29.
177. BEETHOVEN, *Sonatina in G major*

Track 30.
180. SCHUMANN, *Sonata, op. 118², Andante*

Track 31.
182. HANDEL, *Suite XI*

Track 32.
193. BEETHOVEN, *Sonata, op. 53*

Track 33.
201. CHOPIN, *Mazurka, op. 67, no. 2*

Track 34.
202. CHOPIN, *Valse, op. 69, no. 1*

Track 35.
203. CHOPIN, *Valse Brillante, op. 34, no. 3*

Track 36.
205. TCHAIKOVSKY, *Morning Prayer*

Track 37.
207. MOZART, *Sonata, K. 331*

Track 38.
209. HAYDN, *Minuet*

Track 39.
211. HAYDN, *Sonata in C♯ minor, Hob. XVI: 36*

Track 40.
213. CHOPIN, *Mazurka, op. 7, no. 2*

Track 41.
214. HAYDN, *Sonata in G major, Hob. XVI: 39*

Track 42.
215. MOZART, *Sonata, K. 282, Menuet I*

Track 43.
218. HAYDN, *Sonata in E minor, Hob. XVI: 34*

Track 44.
219. MOZART, *Sonata, K. 330*

Track 45.
224. HAYDN, *Sonatina, Hob. XVI: 1*

Track 46.
227. BRAHMS, *Waltz, op. 39, no. 15*

Track 47.
230. BACH, *French Suite in C Minor*

Track 48.
231. BACH, *Wachet auf, ruft uns die Stimme*

Track 49.
232. BACH, *In dulci jubilo*

Track 50.
234. HANDEL, *Menuet*

Track 51.
235. BEETHOVEN, *Sonata, op. 26*

Track 52.
237. BRAHMS, *Waltz, op. 39*

Track 53.
238. HANDEL, *Prelude*

Track 54.
239. BEETHOVEN, *Sonatina in F major*

Track 55.
245. BEETHOVEN, *Contradanse*

Track 56.
250. SCHUMANN, *Carnaval, op. 9: Arlequin*

Track 57.
251. MOZART, *Waltz, K. 567*

Track 58.
257. MOZART, *Concerto in A major, K. 488*

Track 59.
259. BACH, *Ach Gott, vom Himmel sieh' darein*

Track 60.
260. BACH, *Invention No. 13*

Track 61.
262. BRAHMS, *Intermezzo in A major, op. 118, no. 2*

Track 62.
263. CHOPIN, *Prelude, op. 28, no. 20*

Track 63.
269. CHOPIN, *Prelude, op. 28, no. 6*

Track 64.
271. BEETHOVEN, *Bagatelle, op. 119, no. 1*

Track 65.
273. TCHAIKOVSKY, *Mazurka*

Track 66.
276. MOZART, *Sonata, K. 457*

Track 67.
277. BEETHOVEN, *Sonata, op. 109*

Track 68.
279. BEETHOVEN, *Thirty-Two Variations, Var. 30*

Track 69.
285. SCHUBERT, *Sonata, op. 42*

Track 70.
288. GRIEG, *Alfedans, op. 12*

Track 71.
291. MOZART (?), *Adagio*

Track 72.
292. GRANADOS, *Valses Poeticos*

Track 73.
297. TCHAIKOVSKY, *Song Without Words*

Track 74.
299. SCHUBERT, *Waltz*

Track 75.
300. BRAHMS, *Intermezzo, op. 76, no. 4*

Track 76.
301. TCHAIKOVSKY, *The Witch*

Track 77.
302. CHOPIN, *Prelude, op. 28, no. 22*

Track 78.
306. LISZT, *Liebestraum, no. 3*

Track 79.
308. GRIEG, *Solvejg's Lied*

Track 80.
312. SCHUBERT, *Waltz, op. 9, no. 14, D. 365*

Track 81.
317. BEETHOVEN, *Sonata, op. 13*

Track 82.
319. SCRIABIN, *Prelude, op. 13, no. 3*

Track 83.
326. J. STRAUSS, *Artist's Life Waltzes, op. 316, no. 3*

Track 84.
328. BEETHOVEN, *Andante*

Track 85.
329. CHOPIN, *Valse Brillante, op. 34, no. 1*

Track 86.
331. CHOPIN, *Prelude, op. 28, no. 15*

Track 87.
334. GRIEG, *Grandmother's Minuet, op. 68, no. 2*

Track 88.
335. SCHUMANN, *Kinderszenen, op. 15, no. 7: Träumerei*

Track 89.
336. GRIEG, *Wedding Day at Troldhaugen, op. 65, no. 6*

Track 90.
339. CHOPIN, *Mazurka, op. 6, no. 1*

Track 91.
342. BRAHMS, *Variations on a Theme by Handel, var. 20*

Track 92.
346. CHOPIN, *Prelude, op. 28, no. 9*

Track 93.
352. MENDELSSOHN, *Lieder ohne Wörte, op. 30, no. 3*

Track 94.
355. GRIEG, *Erotikon*

Track 95.
356. LISZT, *Il pensieroso, from Années de Pèlerinage*

Track 96.
382. SCRIABIN, *Poem, op. 32, no. 2*

Track 97.
412. DEBUSSY, *Préludes, II: Voiles*

Track 98.
458. DEBUSSY, *Pour le Piano: Sarabande*

Track 99.
459. DEBUSSY, *Préludes, X: La Cathédrale engloutie*

xviii

Preface

In the belief that musical study should focus on the music itself, we have assembled the seventh edition of *Music for Analysis* to provide students with ready access to a far-ranging variety of music. The stylistic and historical breadth, as well as the systematic format, run parallel to our *Techniques and Materials of Music* (Cengage Learning/Schirmer, Seventh Edition, 2008) but also make this anthology ideal for use with many other theory textbooks. Featuring not only 363 excerpts organized by harmonic content, but also 107 complete pieces, this anthology can be used in traditional form and analysis courses as well as in tonal harmony courses. To assist instructors teaching a form course, a separate index lists the complete pieces, which range from small forms to large-scale works and include Mozart and Beethoven piano sonatas.

Features

Music for Analysis moves progressively from the techniques and materials of the common practice period through the twentieth century. Harmonic content forms the organizing principle and builds cumulatively and systematically.

- **We have chosen musical selections that:**
  - Focus clearly on one chord or technique and use music within the range of competent pianists.
  - Illustrate the standard usages and idiomatic procedures of historical periods from the seventeenth through twenty-first centuries.
  - Cover a wide variety of textures and styles, drawing from chamber music, vocal and choral music, keyboard music, and orchestral music–in piano reduction, short score, or full score–and including American popular music and jazz throughout the book.
  - Include excerpts of at least period length as well as many complete works.
- **We believe the anthology is ideal for both tonal harmony courses AND traditional form courses:**
  - The many longer excerpts illustrate small forms such as simple binary, and the numerous complete pieces illustrate all the common large forms.
  - There are clear examples of simple ternary form, examples illustrating variation forms, and complete sonatas for the study of sonata-allegro and rondo form.
  - New for this edition are a complete four-movement Beethoven piano sonata and the prelude to Act I of Tristan und Isolde.
- **We offer discussions of both contrapuntal and contemporary techniques:**
  - Unit 29 contains complete pieces illustrating contrapuntal techniques and includes examples from composers other than Bach. At the end of the unit is a list of a considerable number of contrapuntal examples found throughout the book.
  - Part III presents a clear and systematic illustration of specific techniques and styles found in contemporary music.

- **We provide a number of items to help students in their study of analysis:**
  - Questions for Analysis in each unit are designed to guide study and discussion and remind students of the comprehensive nature of analysis.
  - Model Analyses appear in Units 3, 6, 17, 22, 25, 27, 31 and 37, and prior to Unit 30, and a detailed Checklist and Model Analysis are provided in Appendix A. These show the detail expected at each level of study and reinforce the goal of comprehensive analysis as opposed to simple harmonic analysis and the mere parsing of the phrases.
  - Books dealing with form are listed in Appendix B.
  - The **included audio CD** offers more than 140 examples from the text played on the piano, harpsichord, or organ. For easy reference, each musical selection that can be found on the CD has a CD icon with the appropriate track number next to its title in the text, in the Contents, and Indexes.
  - A detailed Index of Composers and Their Compositions facilitates the study of a particular composer or style; CD icons indicate which of these pieces are played on the included CD.
  - An Index of Complete Pieces also facilitates reference.
- **We provide several items to help busy instructors:**
  - Suggestions for Discussion introduce each of the book's three parts.
  - A Textbook Correlation Chart in Appendix C shows which chapters in this anthology correspond to chapters in the most frequently used theory texts.
  - The audio CD offers more than 140 examples from the text played by Dr. Rosilee Walker Russell, Artist-in-Residence at the University of Arkansas-Fort Smith. The instructor may wish to bring these examples into the classroom to supplement class discussion. For easy reference, each musical selection that can be found on the CD has a CD icon with the appropriate track number next to its title in the text.

New in this Edition

- We have added seven new Model Analyses, including four chromatic tonal excerpts and three from the twentieth century.
- This edition includes two new complete pieces: a four-movement Beethoven piano sonata and the prelude to Act I of *Tristan und Isolde.*
- For easy reference, each musical selection that can be found on the CD has a CD icon with the appropriate track number next to its title in the text.

A Note on the Musical Selections

Movement and measure numbers are provided for excerpts that do not begin a work; longer excerpts and complete pieces have measure numbers provided for ease of reference when discussing the music. Unless otherwise indicated, the excerpt begins on measure 1. In certain cases, a musical selection may contain chords that anticipate later units. In these cases, because we believe that the significance of the selection justifies its inclusion, we provide an analysis of the particular chords. Inevitably, certain selections will suggest alternative analyses; we consider it best to allow the instructor to determine the preferred analysis.

Acknowledgments

We wish again to thank Edward Haymes for his help with the translations. For their very helpful advice toward the seventh edition of *Music for Analysis* we would like to thank Ellon Carpenter, Arizona State University; Robert McMahan, The College of New Jersey; Thom Hasenpflug, Idaho State University; David Heuser, University of Texas at San Antonio; John Hilliard, James Madison University; Robert Knupp, Mississippi College; John Latartara, University of Mississippi; Steve Lindeman, Brigham Young University; Deron McGee, University of Kansas; Michael Murray, Missouri State University; Charles Ruggiero, Michigan State University; and Elizabeth Sayrs, Ohio University.

We also wish to thank Katherine Svistoonoff for her help in revising the textbook correlation chart and the bibliography, Adele Lynch for checking movement and measure numbers, and Nedra Booker for helping with permissions.

T.B.   M.H.   R.N.

Suggestions for Using This Book

1. We urge the class to discuss all aspects of the music being analyzed–not to focus solely, for example, on harmonic content. Constant reference should be made in class discussion to such matters as motivic unity and derivation, melodic construction, counterpoint, cadence and phrase structure, texture, idiom, rhythm, and the like. Suggestions for Discussion introduce each of the book's three parts, and each unit has Questions for Analysis. Model Analyses appear in Units 3, 6, 17, 22, 25, 27, 31 and 37, and prior to Unit 30, and a detailed Checklist and Sample Analysis are provided in Appendix A. These serve as a guide to the teacher and models for the student. Instructors are, of course, free to choose their own analytic approaches and terminologies.

2. It is important to emphasize the organic nature of music so as to avoid limiting class discussion to mere surface description. The interactions of line, rhythm, phrase, and harmony should be investigated. Many complete pieces are provided throughout to allow the students some experience with formal analysis.

3. Such important matters as performance practice, style, and historical context should be discussed in class. Clarification of problems of performance through analysis is often of interest to the student and should be undertaken.

4. Examples of contrapuntal textures are found throughout the anthology. Complete pieces using contrapuntal techniques are designated with an asterisk in the Index of Complete Pieces.

5. The instructor should insist that students listen to the assigned music before doing an analysis and should always play the music in class both before and after discussion. We recommend the use of student performers whenever possible. Further, all of the examples in the anthology are drawn from standard literature. Most keyboard examples, including those for piano, harpsichord, and organ, are included on the accompanying CD. All other examples should be readily available on record or CD in university and college listening laboratories or on the internet.

6. The music in this anthology can be used not only for analysis but also for ear-training, sight-reading, score-reading, and transposition practice.

7. Users of our *Techniques and Materials of Music* (Cengage Learning/ Schirmer, Seventh Edition, 2008) will note that the organization of this anthology closely parallels that of our textbook. The materials provided in Part V of *Techniques and Materials* will be particularly helpful to these instructors; pertinent units in the book include those on cadence and phrase structure, motive, sequence, melody, and small forms.

I. Diatonic Materials

Suggestions for Discussion

Though the music in this section is organized by harmonic vocabulary, it is not enough to simply label the chords with roman numerals and move on. In fact, in those excerpts where the harmonic content is simpler, analysis should focus on all the other aspects of the music, including such basic concepts as harmonic rhythm and the way the voicing and voice-leading is affected by the texture of the music. Harmonic analysis is only the first basic step to understanding and analyzing the structure of a piece of music.

Aspects to Consider

From the very beginning, analysis should include considerations of phrase, period, and cadence; motivic structure; melodic shape; and how all work together to create the musical form. To aid in the analytic process, units are prefaced with questions meant to guide your consideration and analysis of the music. These questions are cumulative and should be considered in all subsequent units.

- Always play the music first, and again after analysis; the *sound* is what matters, and sometimes the eye can be misled. We stress the importance of *hearing* each example in class.
- Always work from large to small. The largest formal units (overall form, structural pitches, cadence, phrase, and periodic structure) should be understood before tackling the details (motives, rhythmic detail, harmony, nonharmonic tones, and so on).
- Always put the music in a context: Who wrote it, when, and what's the nature of the style? What clues about the style does the music give us?
- How does what we have discovered about any particular excerpt or piece help us perform that piece more musically and intelligently?

1. Tonic Triad

Questions for Analysis

1. How is the triad expressed, both melodically and harmonically?
2. How does the texture affect the voicing?
3. Given the lack of a harmonic progression, how are phraselike structures established and articulated?
4. Are successive motives or "phrases" related by sequence, repetition, or other means?

3 Rhythmically Repetition

1. Sonatina in G major, Hob. XVI: 8
I

Haydn

1

2. Sonatina, op. 792, no. 8
I

Czerny

2

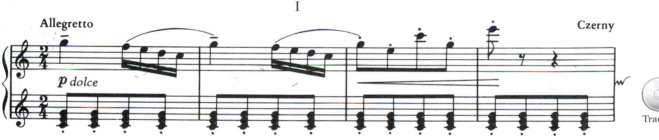

Track 1

3. Le Coq d'Or: Hymn to the Sun
m. 3

Rimsky-Korsakov

3

Note: Movement and measure numbers are given throughout. Where no measure number is given, the excerpt begins on measure 1.

4. Leonora Overture No. 2, op. 72
m. 37

Beethoven

5. Trio, op. 70, no. 2
I

Beethoven

6. Polens Grabgesang, op. 74

Chopin

Moderato (♩ =104)

Von dem Baum im Wet - ter san - ken al - le Blät - ter!

In the storm, all the leaves fell from the tree.

7. Valse (Posthumous)

Chopin

Track 1

8. Symphony No. 5, op. 67
II, m. 230

Beethoven

Andante con moto

9. Carnival

Allegro

Couperin

2. Dominant Triad in Root Position

Questions for Analysis

1. Which dominant chords are clearly cadential? What other devices (melodic, rhythmic) help to establish cadence points?
2. Consider the harmonic voice-leading. How does texture affect the details of the chord connections? Consider particularly the Alberti bass in Example 10 and the arpeggiations in Example 12.

10. Rondo

11. Biblical Sonata No. 1: Victory Dance and Festival

12. Für Elise

Poco moto

Beethoven

pp

Track 2

13. Album for the Young, op. 68: Reiterstück

Kurz und bestimmt

Schumann

pp

cresc.

14. Euryanthe, op. 81: Overture

Weber

Allegro marcato, con molto fuoco

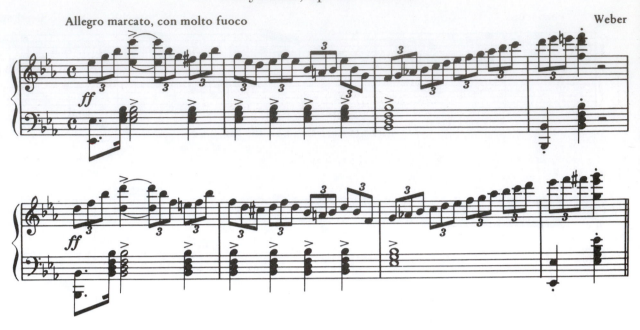

15. Symphony No. 5, op. 67

I, m. 484

Beethoven

Allegro con brio

3. Dominant Seventh and Ninth*
in Root Position

Questions for Analysis

1. Where do tendency tones occur? How are they resolved?
2. How does texture affect the voicing and connection of the chords?
3. Where do cadences occur? How are they established?
4. Does the harmonic rhythm change at cadential points?
5. Do phrases form periods? If so, which type?
6. Are the phrases within each period equal in length?

Model Analysis

Beethoven, *Piano Sonata, op. 31, no.2*

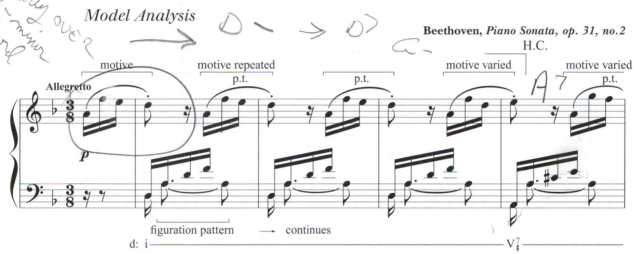

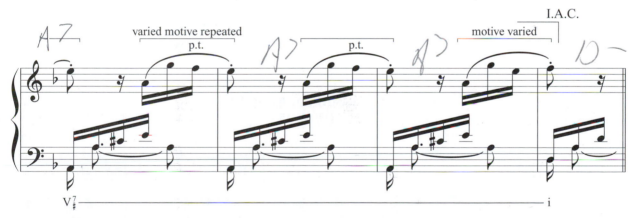

Observations:

A. Form: two four-measure phrases, a⎸a'⎸ forming a period in which the same motive appears in both phrases but is altered in the second phrase to fit the underlying harmony. The structural harmony supports the two-part structure: i →V answered and balanced by V→i.

B. The excerpt is highly continuous in its rhythmic flow and highly unified in its motivic material (one motivic idea and one figuration pattern).

*For additional examples of the dominant ninth, see Part II, Unit 26.

C. Harmonic rhythm is slow and regular:

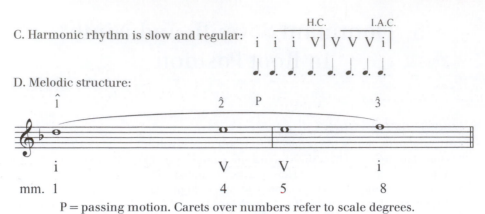

D. Melodic structure:

P = passing motion. Carets over numbers refer to scale degrees.

E. See also Appendix A, p. 503.

16. German Dance

17. Sonata, K. 332
III, m. 15

18. Wiegenlied, op. 98, no. 2

Schubert

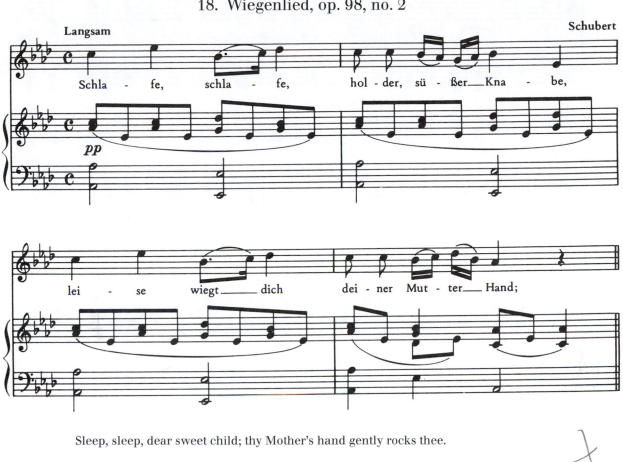

Langsam

Schla - fe, schla - fe, hol - der, sü - ßer Kna - be,

lei - se wiegt dich dei - ner Mut - ter Hand;

Sleep, sleep, dear sweet child; thy Mother's hand gently rocks thee.

19. Rigoletto, Act I, no. 2

Verdi

Allegretto

6

(Duke) con eleganza

Que-sta o quel - la per me pa - ri so - no a quan -

t'al - - tre d'in - tor - no, _____ d'in - tor - no mi ve - do,

del mio co - re _____ l'im - pe - ro non ce - do _____

_____ me - glio ad u - na, _____ che ad al - tra bel - tà.

This one or that one, it's all the same to me. As to the others I see around me,
I don't yield my heart more to one beauty than to another.

---

20. Sonata in E major, Hob. XVI: 13
III, m. 15

Presto

Haydn

Track 3

21. Symphony No. 4, op. 60
I, m. 177

Beethoven

22. Oberon: Overture
m. 22

Weber

23. Ländler

Schubert

Track 3

24. Valses Nobles, op. 77

Schubert

Track 3

16   PART I. DIATONIC MATERIALS

25. Valse

Mozart

[I⁶₄]

4. Subdominant Triad in Root Position

Questions for Analysis

1. What is the explanation for all the accidentals in Example 30?
2. What is the formal design of the complete pieces (Examples 33 and 34)?
3. How does motive contribute to the form of these pieces?

26. Bergamasca

26

Track 4

27. Faschingsschwank aus Wien, op. 26, no. 3: Scherzino
m. 86

27

Track 4

28. Mazurka, op. 17, no. 1

Chopin

Track 4

29. Egmont Overture, op. 84
m. 82

Beethoven

30. Rigoletto, Act I, no. 7

Verdi

Gilda: What sadness! what sadness! have rung such bitter tears.
Rigoletto: You alone remain in misery . . .

31. Impromptu, op. 90, no. 4, D. 899
m. 88

Allegretto

Schubert

Track 4

32. Look for the Silver Lining

Burthen *(slowly)*

Kern

Look for_____ the sil - ver lin - ing_____

p *molto legato*

_____ When - e'er a cloud ap - pears in the

blue._____

33. Seven Country Dances, no. 7

Allegro

Beethoven

Track 4

34. Ländler

Schubert

Track 4

5. Cadential Tonic Six-Four Chord

Questions for Analysis

1. Do any of the examples in this unit contain phrase groups or double periods?
2. How is the cadential tonic six-four chord introduced and resolved? Consider aspects of doubling and voice-leading as well as those of rhythm and meter.

35. Valses Sentimentales, op. 50, no. 18
m. 10

Schubert

Track 5

36. Mazurka, op. 24, no. 3

Chopin

37. Lucia di Lammermoor, Act II, no. 6
m. 344

Donizetti

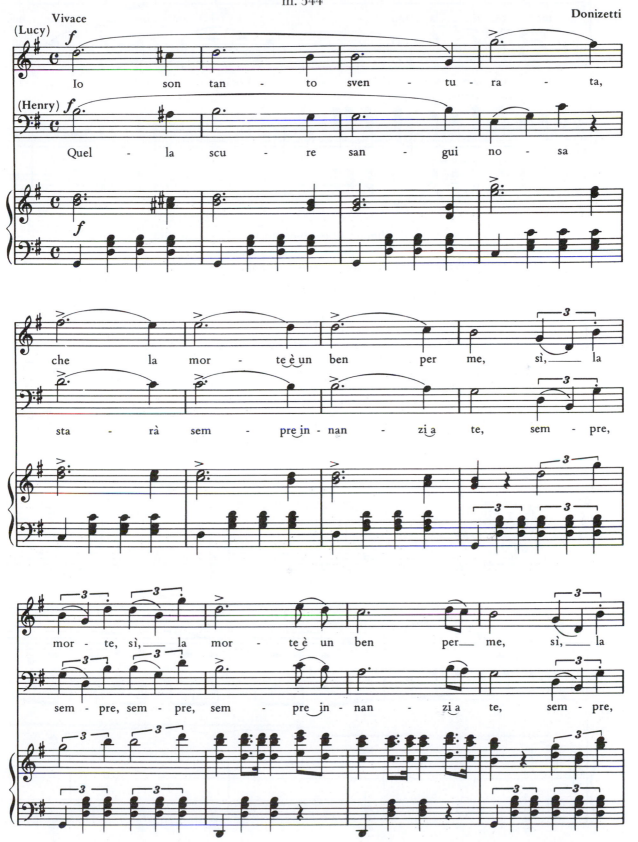

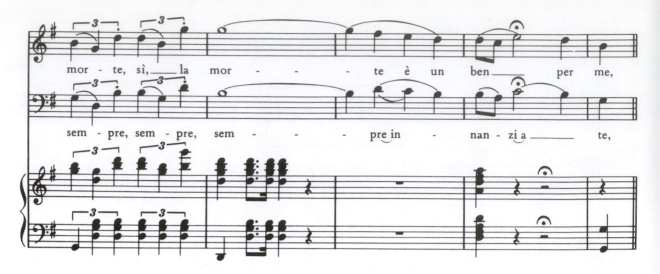

Lucy: I am so wretched that death is a blessing for me, yes, death is a blessing
for me.
Henry: That bloody axe will always be before you.

---

38. Trio, op. 97

Beethoven

6. Tonic, Subdominant, and Dominant Triads in First Inversion

Questions for Analysis

1. Where do chords in inversion occur?
2. How does the inversion of these chords affect the bass line?

Model Analysis

Beethoven, *Dance*

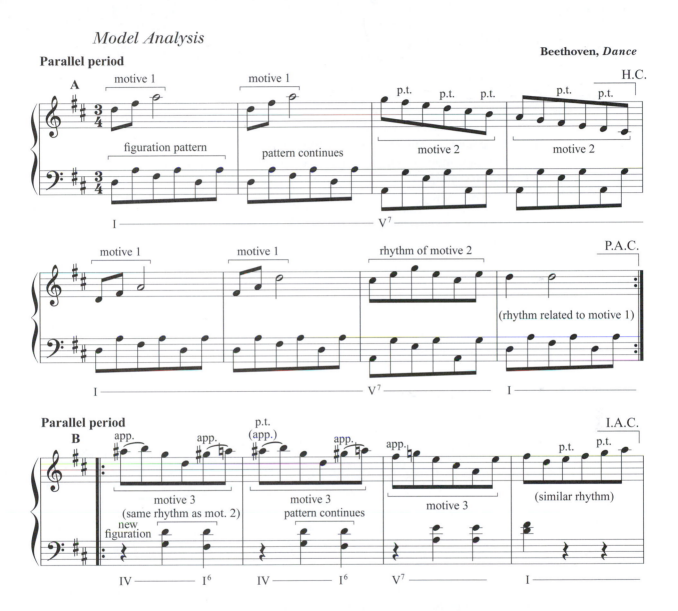

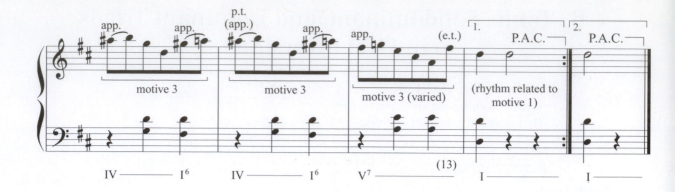

IV ——— I⁶   IV ——— I⁶   V⁷ ———   (13)   I ——— I ———

Observations:

A. Form: simple binary. ||:A:||:B:||

B. Each section is a parallel period consisting of two four-measure phrases.

C. There is new motivic material and a new figuration in the B section.

D. Harmonic rhythm

   1. A section: slow

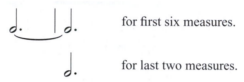 for first six measures.

for last two measures.

   2. B section: faster, slowing at the cadence

 each phrase.

E. Background rhythmic unit: eighth note motion throughout, passing from the accompanimental figuration in the A section to the melodic material in the B section and coming to rest in the final measure.

F. Melodic structure.

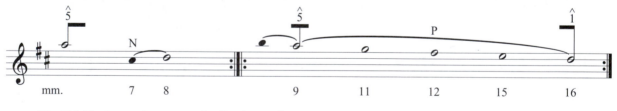

mm.   7   8   9   11   12   15   16

N = Neighboring motion   P = Passing motion

   G. See also Appendix A on page 549.

39. Lobt Gott, ihr Christen, allzugleich

Bach

Track 6

40. Bastien und Bastienne, K. 46B, no. 9

Mozart

Moderato

(Bastien)

Geh'! du sagst mir ein-e

Fa - bel;   geh'! du sagst mir ein-e   Fa - bel;   Ba - sti - en - ne

11

trü - get nicht Ba - sti - en - ne trü - get nicht.

Go on! You're telling me a fib. Bastienne, don't deceive me.

41. Sonata, K. 332
I, m. 145

Allegro

Mozart

Track 6

42. Sonata in D major, Hob. XVI: 37
III, m. 114

Presto ma non troppo

Haydn

Track 6

*See Chapter 9.

43. Abendempfindung, K. 523

Mozart

It's evening. The sun has faded.

44. Symphony No. 5, op. 67

IV

Beethoven

45. Fidelio, Act I, no. 9
m. 34

Beethoven

46. Sonata, K. 570

Mozart

Track 6

Which notes in the bass line of the example below are clearly roots or thirds and which are merely passing tones?

47. Elijah, op. 70, no. 29
m. 70

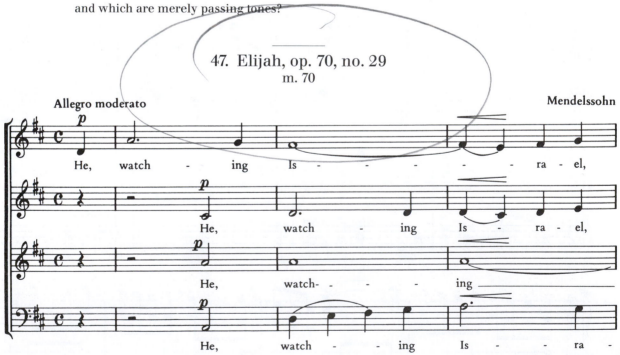

Mendelssohn

He, watch - ing Is - - - - ra - el,

He, watch - ing Is - ra - el,

He, watch- - - ing

He, watch - - ing Is - ra -

slum - - - - - bers___ not, nor sleeps.

slum - - - - bers not, nor sleeps.

___ slum - - - bers not, nor sleeps.

el, _____ slum - bers not, nor sleeps.

48. Le Petit Rien

m. 67

Allegro

Couperin

Track 6

ii

49. Les Fifres

Vif

Dandrieu

7. Supertonic Triad

Questions for Analysis

1. How is the supertonic triad introduced and resolved? Which note is doubled in the ii6?
2. Where do cadences occur? How are they established? Do phrases form periods?

50. Dir, dir, Jehovah, will ich singen

Anon.

51. Waltz, op. 9, no. 3, D. 365

Schubert

52. Six Variations on "Nel cor più non mi sento", WoO 70

Beethoven

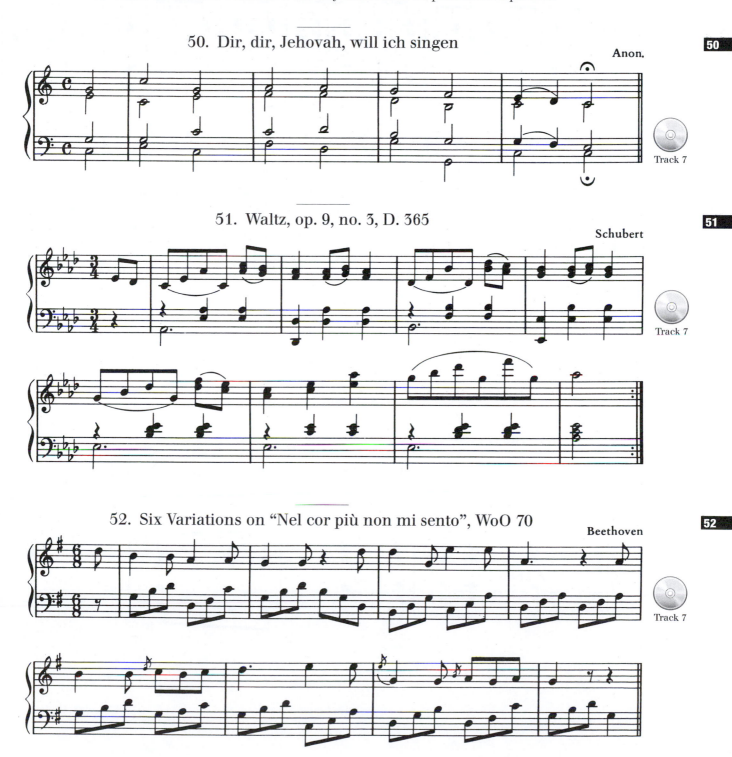

Track 7

Track 7

Track 7

53. Die Zauberflöte, K. 620, Act II, no. 21
m. 584

Mozart

Allegro
(Papageno)

Klin - get, Glöck - chen, klin - get! schafft mein Mäd - chen her,

klin - get, Glöck - chen, klin - get! bringt mein Mäd - chen her,

Ring, little bells, ring. Bring my maiden here.

54. Zwei Leichen

Allegretto (♩ = 100)

Chopin

1. Zwei die sich lieb - ten, die durf - ten's nicht ge - ste - hen,

muss - ten sich mei - den und von ein - an - der ge - hen.

V7/iv   ii⌀6/5

Two lovers were kept from each other and had to part.

55. Trio, op. 121A

56. Rigoletto, Act II, no. 14

Allegro vivo

Verdi

Yes, revenge, terrible revenge, is this soul's only desire.

57. Mazurka, op. 33, no. 2

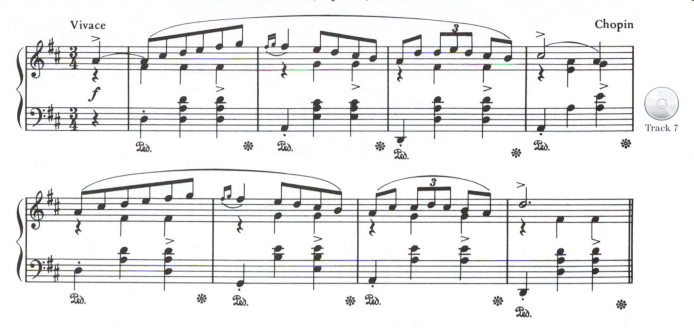

Vivace   Chopin

Track 7

58. Sonata in E minor, Hob. XVI: 34
II

Adagio   Haydn

8. Inversions of the Dominant Seventh Chord

Questions for Analysis

1. Where do tendency tones occur? How are they resolved?
2. Do inversons of dominant sevenths occur at cadence points? If so, how does this affect the relative strength of the cadence?

---

59. Nun danket alle Gott

J. C. F. Bach

Track 8

---

60. Sonata in C major, Hob. XVI: 35

I

Haydn

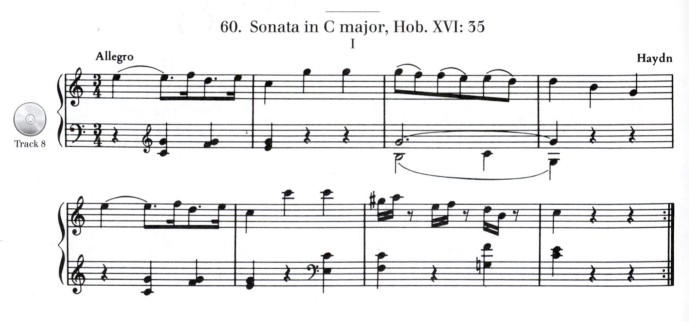

Track 8

---

61. Le donne sur balcone

Paisiello

Le don-ne sul bal - co - ne   so be-ne in-do-vi -

nar.   I gio-va-ni al can-to - ne   so me-glio stuz-zi - car.

The ladies on the balcony I know well how to evaluate,
The young men on the corner I know better how to tease.

———

62. Quartet, K. 464

Allegro   Mozart

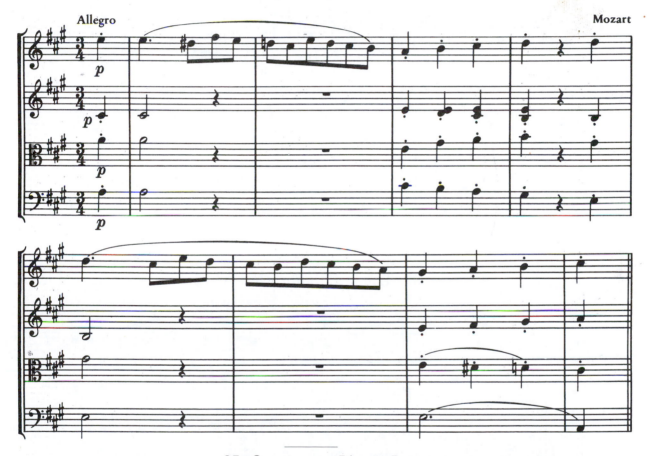

———

63. Sonata, op. 31, no. 3
II

Allegretto vivace   Beethoven

Track 8

64. Sarabande I, vol. I

Rameau

ii°7

65. Trio in C major, Hob. XV: 3

Haydn*

Violin

Cello

Piano

*Possibly by Pleyel.

66. Sonatina, op. 20, no. 1

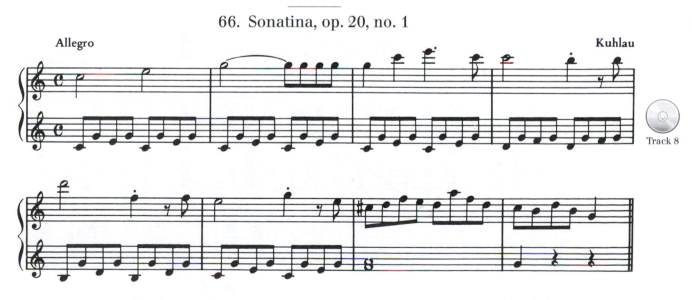

Track 8

67. Symphony No. 2, op. 36

Allegro molto

Beethoven

68. Minuet in C

Moderato

Beethoven

Track 8

5

3rd in BASS G7/B

C♯/E

11

*See Part I, Unit 9.

9. Linear (Embellishing) Six-Four Chords

Questions for Analysis

1. Which chords are clearly functional? Which are linear?
2. What combinations of nonharmonic tones create the linear chords?

69. Concerto No. 1 for Piano, op. 15

Beethoven

70. Valses Sentimentales, op. 50, no. 1, D. 779

Schubert

Track 9

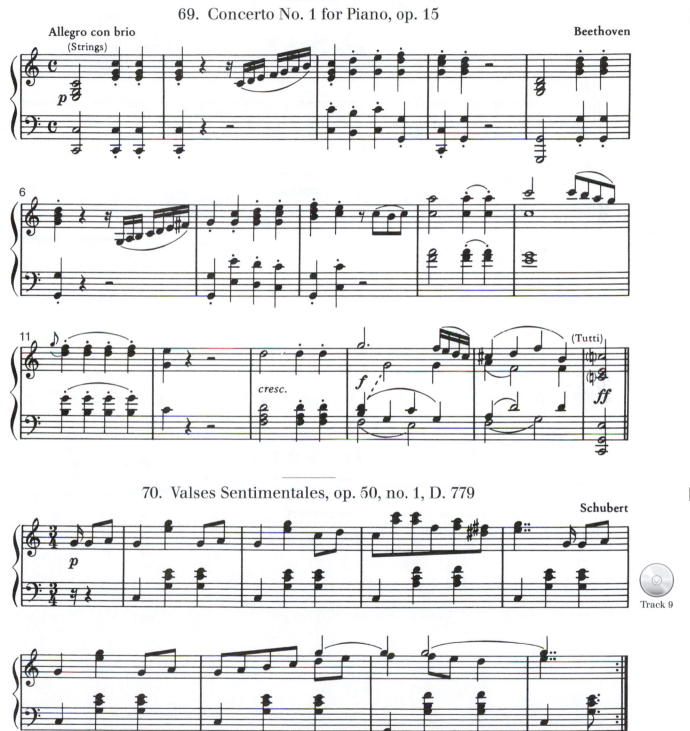

71. Rondo, K. 485

Mozart

72. Quartet, op. 3, no. 5

Andante cantabile

Haydn

73. Waltz, op. 9, no. 1, D. 365

Schubert

Track 9

74. Sonatina, op. 88, no. 3
III

Kuhlau

75. Symphony No. 35, K. 385

Mozart

Menuetto (Trio)

76. Sonatina in G major
I, m. 25

Moderato   Beethoven

mf

Track 9

77. Symphony No. 7, op. 92
I, m. 63

Vivace   Beethoven

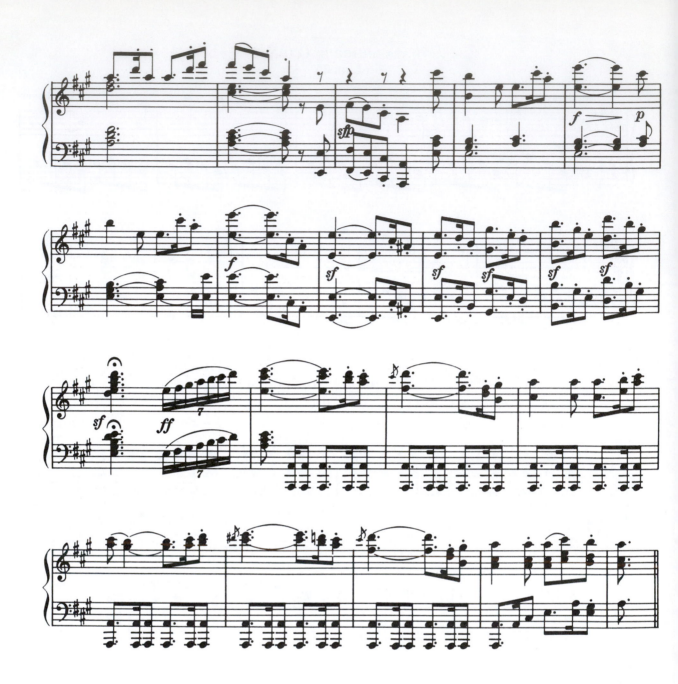

78. Symphony No. 41, K. 551
I

Allegro vivace   Mozart

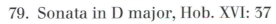

79. Sonata in D major, Hob. XVI: 37
I

Allegro con brio   Haydn

Track 9

80. Contradanse

Allegro

Beethoven

81. Passacaglia

Buxtehude

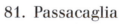

---

82. Symphony No. 3, op. 55
III, m. 167

---

83. Faust, Act I, no. 6

Like the gentle breeze . . .

84. H.M.S. Pinafore, "I'm Called Little Buttercup"

Allegretto
Song. Mrs. Cripps

Sullivan

I'm called lit – tle But – ter – cup, Dear lit – tle But – ter – cup,

Though I could ne – ver tell why; But still I'm called But – ter – cup,

$$V_{5/ii}^6$$

Poor lit – tle But – ter – cup, Sweet lit – tle But – ter – cup I.

9. LINEAR (EMBELLISHING) SIX-FOUR CHORDS   55

10. Submediant and Mediant Triads

Questions for Analysis

1. How are the submediant and mediant triads introduced and resolved? Which chord tone is doubled?
2. Where do sequences occur? Analyze in detail.

---

85. Herzliebster Jesu, was hast du verbrochen

Crüger

Track 10

---

86. Dir, dir, Jehovah, will ich singen

Anon.

Track 10

ii $^6_5$

---

87. Schmücke dich, o liebe Seele

Bach

Track 10

88. Bastien und Bastienne, K. 46B, no. 1
m. 11

Mozart

Andante, un poco adagio
(Bastienne)

Mein lieb - ster Freund hat mich ver - las - sen, mit ihm ist Schlaf__ und

Ruh'   da - hin,   mit ihm ist Schlaf und__ Ruh'   da - hin.

My dear friend has forsaken me, sleep and rest have left with him.

89. Sonata, K. 545

Mozart

Rondo

Track 10

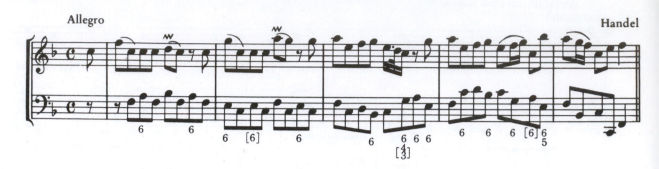

90. Sonata in F for Flute and Continuo
II

Allegro

Handel

91. Rigoletto, Act I, no. 1

Allegro con brio

Verdi

92. Symphony No. 4, op. 98
IV

Allegro giocoso

Brahms

93. Sonata for Violin and Continuo, op. 5, no. 9
II, m. 5

Corelli

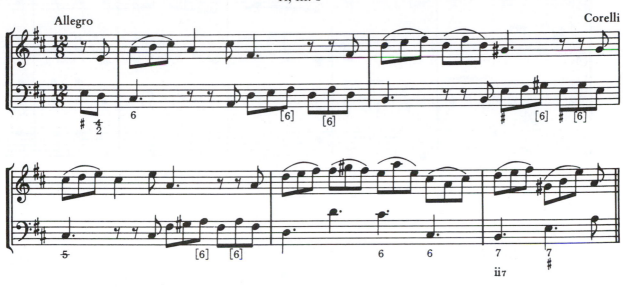

94. Quartet in D major, D. 74

Schubert

*This implies V7/IV.

95. Trio, op. 1, no. 3

Beethoven

96. Sonata, K. 283

97. Menuet

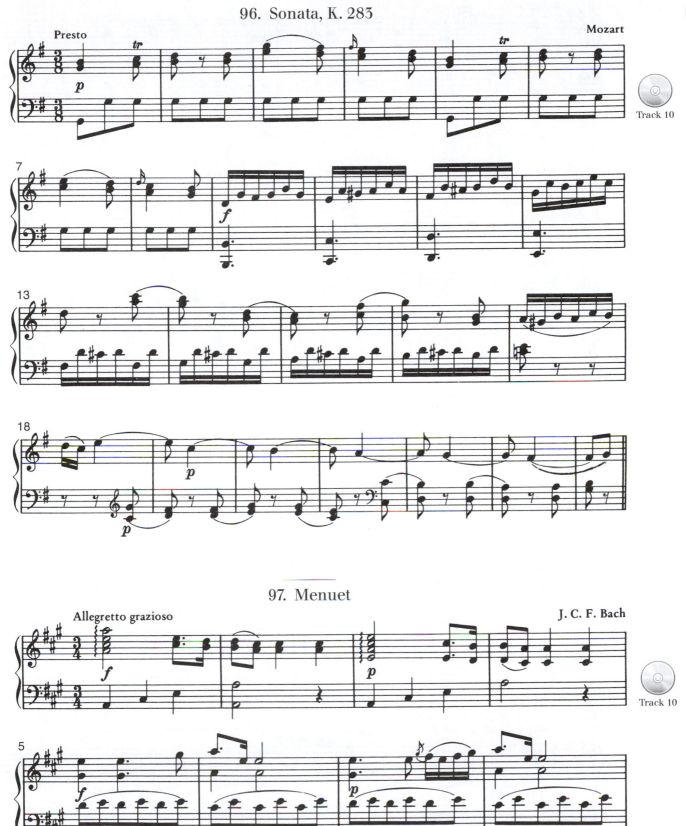

Track 10

98. Au joli bois je m'en vais

Tessier

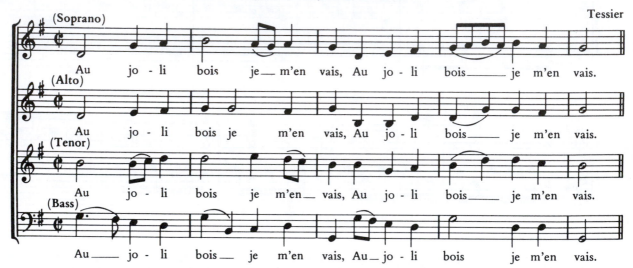

To the pretty woods I go.

99. Der Rosenkavalier, Act III
Reh. 297, m. 3

Strauss

daß wir zwei bei-ei-nan-der sein, bei-ei-nand' für

und daß wir bei-ei-nan-der sein! Geht all's sonst wie ein

al-le Zeit und E - - - - - -wig-keit.

Traum da-hin vor mei - - - - - -nem Sinn.

Sophie: It is a dream, it can't really be true that we two are together for all time
  and eternity.
Octavian: Know that I love only you and that we two are together. Everything
  passes before my sight as a dream.

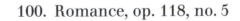

100. Romance, op. 118, no. 5

Andante   Brahms

espressivo

Track 10

101. Phantasiestücke, op. 12, no. 4: Grillen
m. 17

Mit humor

Schumann

Track 10

102. Im Abendroth (Posthumous)

Langsam, feierlich

Schubert

con Ped.

O, wie schön ist dei - ne Welt, Va - ter, wenn sie gol - den

strah - let,   wenn dein Glanz her - nie - der fällt

und   den Staub mit Schim-mer ma - let;

O, how beautiful is Thy world, Father, when it shines like gold, when Thy brightness falls upon it and paints the dust with shimmering brightness.

---

103. Symphony in C major ("The Great")

Schubert

*Refer also to Unit 11.

11. Leading Tone Triad

Questions for Analysis

1. How is the leading tone triad introduced and resolved?
2. Where do cadences occur? How are they established? Do phrases form periods? Of what type?

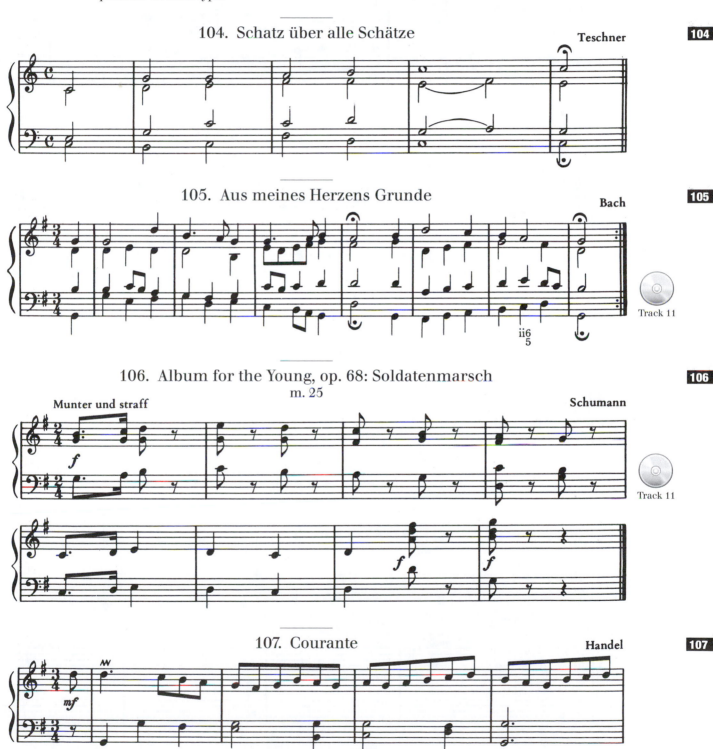

104. Schatz über alle Schätze

Teschner

105. Aus meines Herzens Grunde

Bach

Track 11

106. Album for the Young, op. 68: Soldatenmarsch
m. 25

Munter und straff

Schumann

Track 11

107. Courante

Handel

108. Sonata in E♭ major, Hob. XVI: 49
I

Haydn

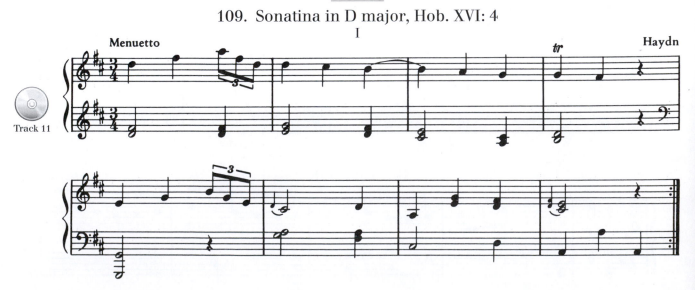

109. Sonatina in D major, Hob. XVI: 4
I

Haydn

110. Sonata, K. 280
I, m. 131

111. La Joyeuse

Daquin

Légèrement

12. Variant Qualities of Diatonic Triads

Questions for Analysis

1. Identify all scalar variants and modally borrowed chords.
2. Carefully analyze the qualities of all chords in this unit.

SCALAR VARIANTS IN MINOR

112. Herr, ich habe mißgehandelt

Bach

112

113. Chaconne

Pachelbel

113

114. Fantasie No. 8

Telemann

Vivace

114

---

115. Pavana "The Earle of Salisbury"

Byrd

iv 6
5

---

116. Folia

A. Scarlatti

Track 12

117. Minuet

Mattheson

Track 12

118. Sonata, K. 310

III, m. 211

Presto

Mozart

Track 12

119. La Traviata, Act I, no. 4
m. 16

Andantino

Alfredo

Verdi

Di quel - l'a - mor, quel - l'a - mor____ ch'è pal - pi - to

del - l'u - ni - ver - so, del - l'u - ni - ver - so in - te - ro,

mi - ste - ri - o - so, mi - ste - ri - o - so,al - te - ro,

croce, cro-ce e de - li - zia, cro-ce e de - li - zia, de-li-zia al cor.

Love, which is the moving force of the entire universe,
The mysterious one, the proud one, the cross and delight to the heart.

120. Linda di Chamounix, "O Luce di quest' anima"

Donizetti

O lu - ce di quest' a - ni - ma, de - li - zia a - mor e vi - ta,

la no - stra sor - te u - ni - ta in ter - ra in ciel sa - rà,

Oh, light of this soul, delight and love and life, our fate will be united on earth
and in heaven.

121. Sonata for Violin and Piano, K. 306

m. 51

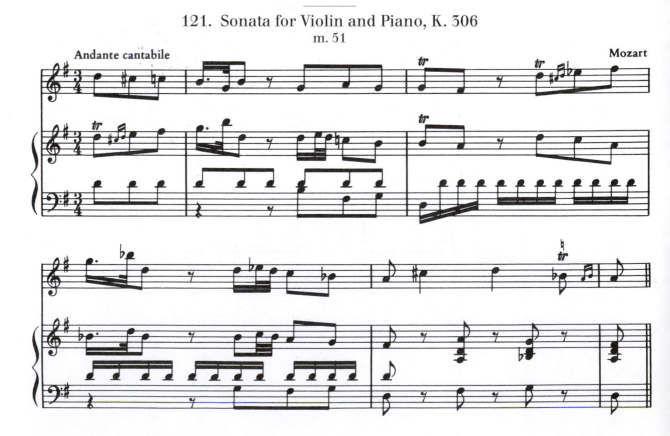

122. Sonatina in C major, Hob. XVI: 7
III. m. 26

Allegro

Haydn

Track 12

123. Aufenthalt

Schubert

Non troppo vivace, con fuoco

Rau - schen - der Strom,   brau - sen - der Wald,   star - ren - der

Rushing stream, blustering wood, immobile rocks, my abode.

124. Der Wanderer

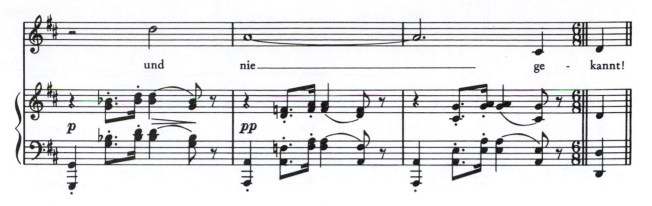

und ____ nie _____ ge - kannt!

Where are you, my beloved country? Sought for, yearned for, and never known!

---

125. Symphony No. 3, op. 90
II, m. 128

Brahms

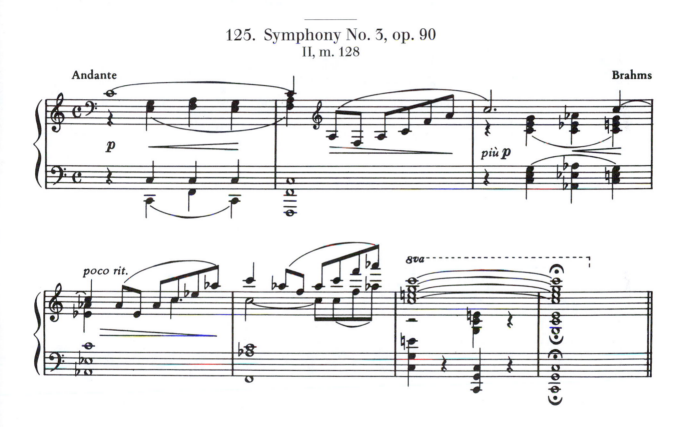

126. Il Trovatore, Act II, no. 11
m. 50

Verdi

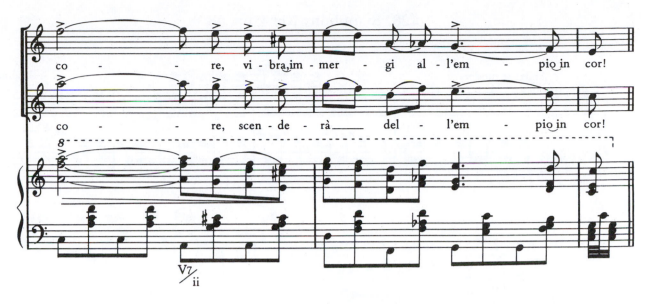

Azucena: Plunge this blade up to the hilt into the heart of the cruel one. Strike!
Manrico: Yes, I swear it. This blade will descend into the heart of the cruel one.

127. Symphony No. 5, op. 67
III, m. 27

Beethoven

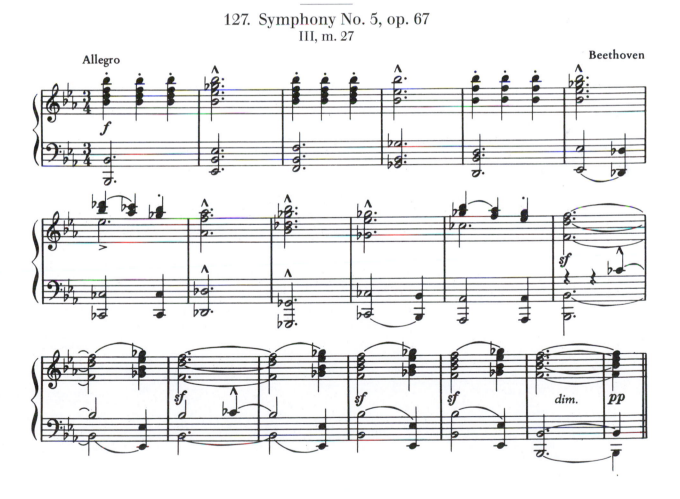

128. Symphony No. 4, op. 98
II

Andante moderato   Brahms

13. Supertonic Seventh Chord

Questions for Analysis

1. How is the seventh of the ii7 introduced and resolved?
2. Where do cadences occur? Do phrases form periods?

129. Herr, wie du willst, so schick's mit mir

Anon.

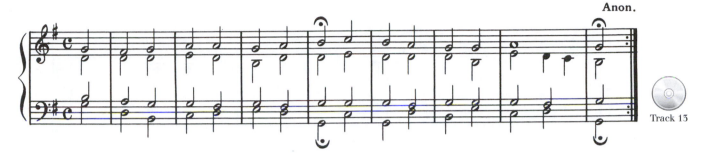

Track 13

130. Straf' mich nicht in deinem Zorn
I

Bach

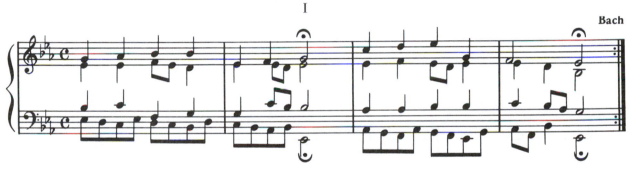

131. Sonata in A♭ major, Hob. XVI: 46
III

Presto

Haydn

13. SUPERTONIC SEVENTH CHORD   83

132. Voegtersang, op. 12, No. 3

Molto andante e semplice

Grieg

Track 13

133. Symphony No. 6, op. 68
V, m. 237

Allegretto

Beethoven

134. Quartet, op. 168, D. 112
III

MENUETTO
Allegro

Schubert

135. Sonata, K. 310
I, m. 129

Allegro maestoso

Mozart

Track 13

136. Ständchen

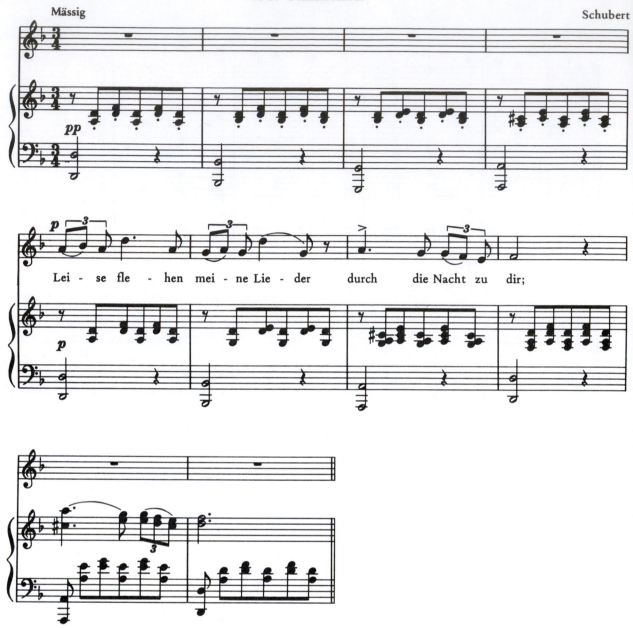

My songs float lightly through the night to you.

137. Symphony No. 2, op. 36
II, m. 246

Larghetto

Beethoven

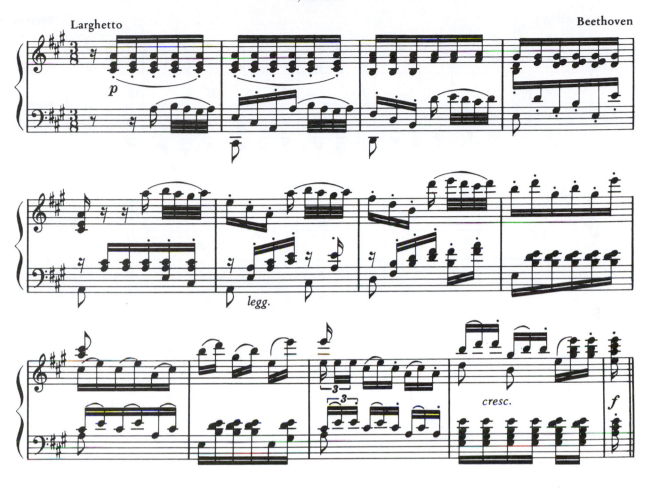

138. Sonata, op. 14, no. 2
I

Allegro

Beethoven

Track 13

139. Symphony No. 6, op. 68
III, m. 53

Beethoven

140. Carmen, Act II: Entr'acte

Allegro moderato

Bizet

141. Blue Moon

Slowly, with feeling

Rodgers

Blue Moon! _____ Now I'm no long-er a-lone ___

_____ With-out a dream in my heart, _____

13. SUPERTONIC SEVENTH CHORD   89

With - out a love of my own

14. Leading Tone Seventh Chord

Questions for Analysis

1. What is the quality of the leading tone seventh chord in each example? Is the chord diatonic or altered?
2. How is the seventh introduced and resolved?
3. Where do cadences occur? How are they established?

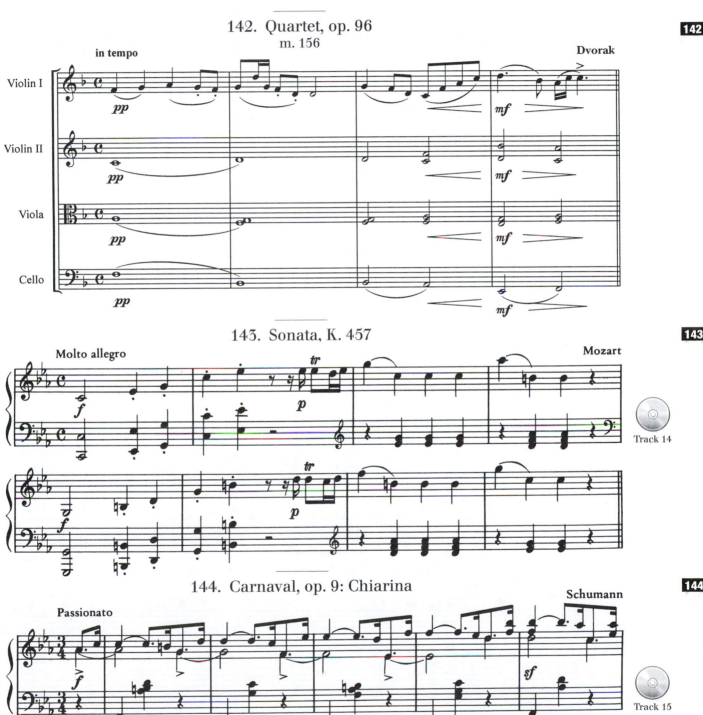

142. Quartet, op. 96

m. 156

Dvorak

143. Sonata, K. 457

Mozart

Track 14

144. Carnaval, op. 9: Chiarina

Schumann

Track 15

14. LEADING TONE SEVENTH CHORD   91

145. Ballade, op. 10, no. 4
m. 89

Brahms

146. Sonata for Flute and Continuo

Handel

147. Allegro

Haydn (?)

Track 17

148. Trio in G major, Hob. XV: 25
m. 121

149. Requiem, K. 626: Offertorium

Lord Jesus Christ, King of Glory! Free the souls of all the faithful from death's bonds.

150. Sonatina in G major, Hob. XVI: 11
III, m. 44

Haydn

Track 18

151. Judas Maccabaeus, Part III: no. 53, Introduction

Handel

152. Das Rheingold, scene 1

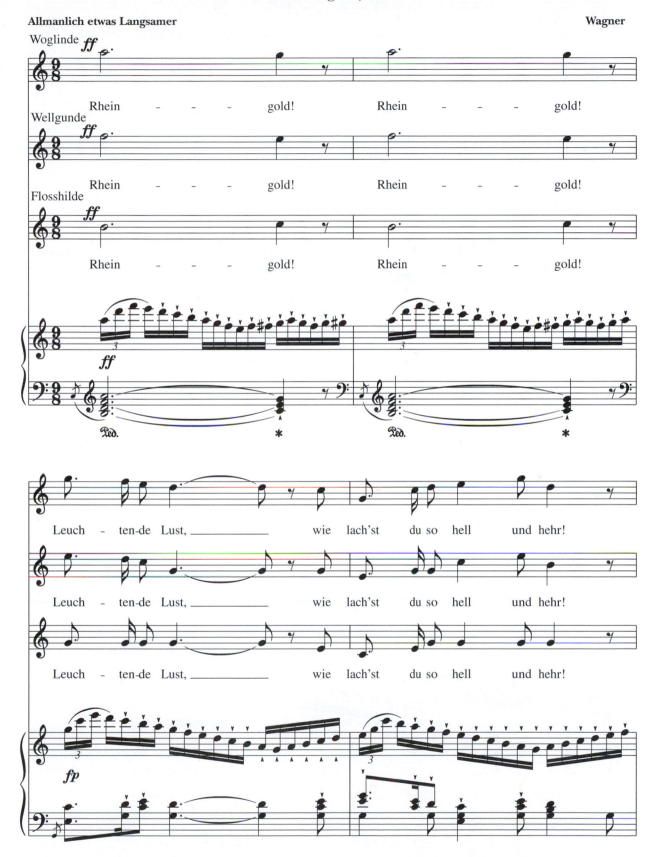

Glü - hen-der Glanz _____ ent - gleis - set dir weih-lich im Wag!

Glü - hen-der Glanz _____ ent - gleis - set dir weih-lich im Wag!

Glü - hen-der Glanz _____ ent - gleis - set dir weih-lich im Wag!

hei - a ja - hei! _____

hei - a ja - hei! _____

hei - a ja - hei! _____

Rhine gold! Rhine gold!
Bright joy!
How you laugh, so clear and majestic
Glowing luster, you glisten daringly.

153. Orphée, Act I, no. 1
m. 15

Moderato

Gluck

Ah! dans ce bois _____ tran - quille et som - bre,

Ah! dans ce bois tran - quille et som - bre,

Ah! dans ce bois tran - quille et som - bre,

Ah! dans ce bois tran - quille et som - bre,

Eu - ri - di - ce, si ton om - bre,

Eu - ri - di - ce, si ton om - bre,

Eu - ri - di - ce, si ton om - bre,

Eu - ri - di - ce, si ton om - bre,

si ton om - bre nous en - tend, _____
si ton om - bre nous en - tend,
si ton om - bre nous en - tend, _____
si ton om - bre nous en - tend,

$vii°7/V$

Ah, in this dark and quiet wood, Euridice, if thy spirit hears us . . .

154. Aria con Variazioni, Leçon No. 1

II

Handel

155. Fantasia, 1er Dozzina, no. 5
II

Grave   Telemann

156. Sonata for Violin and Piano, K. 306

Mozart

15. Other Diatonic Seventh Chords

Questions for Analysis

1. How are the chord sevenths introduced and resolved?
2. Where do sequences occur? Analyze both harmonically and melodically (motivically).
3. Discuss the texture of all the examples. Which are predominately homophonic and which predominately polyphonic?

157. O Ewigkeit, du Donnerwort

Bach

Track 19

158. Rondo, K. 494
m. 95

Andante

Mozart

159. Kinderstück, op. 72, no. 1

Allegro moderato

Mendelssohn

Track 20

15. OTHER DIATONIC SEVENTH CHORDS   103

160. Fantasie

Pachelbel

161. Sonata for Flute and Continuo

Handel

162. Leçon No. 2, Menuet

Handel

163. Symphony No. 4, op. 36
II

Andantino in modo di canzona

Tchaikovsky

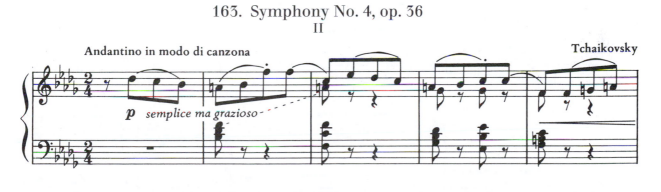

p semplice ma grazioso

164. French Suite in D minor

16. Complete Pieces for Analysis I

Checklist for Analysis

✓ *Subjective aspects, including affect, mood, expression:* How are these achieved?

✓ *Stylistic aspects:* What features of the music tell us who wrote it?

✓ *Form:* Overall form, cadences, phases, periodic structure if any.

✓ *Rhythm:* Meter, rhythmic patterns (motives), special effects. How is continuity achieved, and where are the resting points?

✓ *Harmony:* Harmonic details, including cadences, chords, inversions, nonharmonic tones. Which are the structural chords? Which are embellishing or linear?

✓ *Line:* Structural pitches, motives, cadence figures; placement of climax, if any.

✓ *Counterpoint and voice-leading:* How do the outer voices relate to each other in terms of intervals, intervallic patterns, relative motion, and so on? Are all tendency tones conventionally resolved?

✓ *All aspects of pattern:* Accompaniment patterns, harmonic and motivic patterns; patterns of nonharmonic tones.

165. Minuet

Track 22

166. Dance

Schubert

Track 23

167. German Dance, op. 33, no. 12

Schubert

Track 24

168. Scottish Dance

Beethoven

Track 25

169. Rigadoon

Purcell

170. Minuet

Rameau

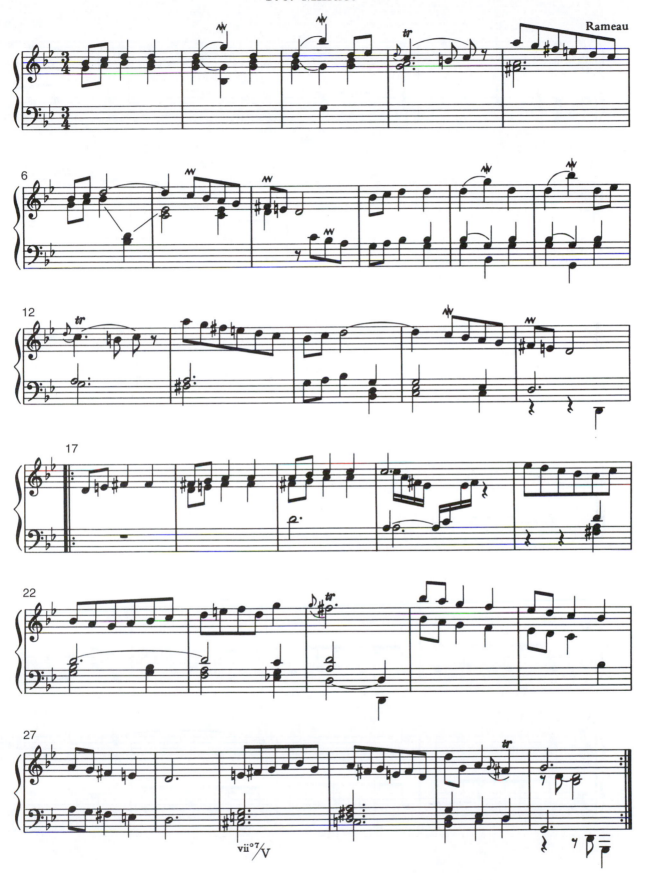

vii°7/V

171. Passacaglia

Witt

*Additional variations follow.

172. Norsk, op. 12, No. 6

Grieg

II. Chromatic Materials

Suggestions for Discussion

This section introduces the chromatic vocabulary (secondary dominants and other altered chords) and techniques of modulation. As with the previous section, it is essential that your analysis go beyond mere labeling of key and chords. Particularly with the modulating examples, consider the way in which the first key is established and the devices by which the composer effects the modulation to the new key. All aspects of formal design must be considered, including motive, figuration pattern, phrase, period, cadence, and harmonic rhythm. Be attentive to such details as sequence, repetition, and contrapuntal relationships.

Additional Aspects to Consider

- All instances of chromaticism in a line: Are they functional (chord members) or nonharmonic; are they used sequentially and/or motivically?
- All chromatically altered chords: Are they functional or linear; what diatonic chords do they replace; what sequential or other patterns do they form? Where are they used within the piece?
- Again, we direct your attention to the *Suggestions for Using This Book* on page xxii and reiterate the importance of *hearing* the music in class and of discussing *all* the musical elements and their interactions.

17. Secondary (Applied, Borrowed) Dominants

Model Analysis   **Beethoven**, *Piano Sonata, op. 10, No. 3*

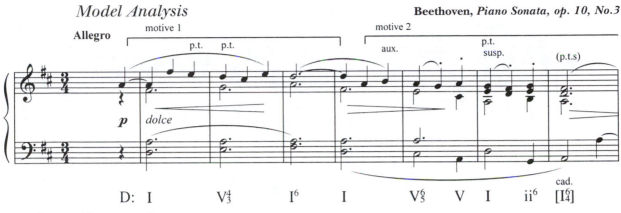

D: I   V$^4_3$ I^6 I   V$^6_5$ V   I   ii^6 [I$^6_4$]

Structural harmony: I →

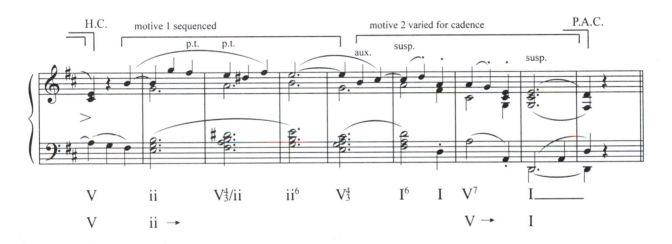

V   ii   V$^4_3$/ii   ii^6 V$^4_3$ I^6 I V^7 I_____

V   ii →   V →   I

Observations:

A. Form: two eight-measure phrases, a | a', forming a sequential period.
   The underlying structural harmony supports the two-section parallel
   structure.

   H.C.   P.A.C.
   I   V | ii   V I |

B. The harmonic rhythm is quite regular: one chord per measure, except
   speeding up approaching the first cadence.
C. There appear to be two motivic gestures, a rising idea and a falling one
   (building and then releasing tension through shape of line). The melodic
   line (mm. 1-3) is supported by a rising bass line, both treated sequentially
   in the second phrase (mm. 9-11). Study the bass line in terms of the harmonic implications of its scale degrees.
D. The structural upper voice and bass lines are somewhat complex in this
   excerpt. You may wish to make a linear reduction of both.
E. See also Appendix A, pp. 503.

Questions for Analysis

1. How are secondary dominants introduced? Which are the tendency tones and how are they resolved?
2. Where do cadences occur? Analyze each as to type.

173. Trio, op. 1, no. 1

Beethoven

174. Sonata, K. 281

III

Mozart

Track 27

175. Impromptu, op. 142, no. 3

Schubert

Track 28

176. Trio in D major
I, m. 178

Haydn

177. Sonatina in G major
II

Beethoven

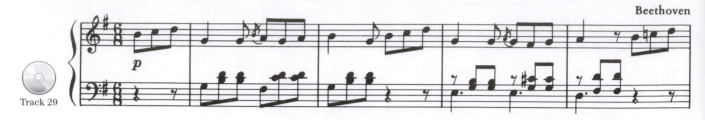

Track 29

178. Oberon: Overture
m. 65

Allegro con fuoco

Weber

dolce

179. Trio, op. 1, no. 1

Beethoven

180. Sonata, op. 118ᶜ, Andante

Ausdrucksvoll

Schumann

Track 30

181. Symphony No. 1, op. 21

Adagio molto

Beethoven

Allegro con brio

182. Suite XI

Sarabande

Handel

Track 31

183. Arabeske, op. 18

Leicht und zart

Schumann

184. Symphony No. 4, op. 60

185. Widmung, op. 25, no. 1

Grab, in das hin-ab ich e - wig mei-ne Kum - mer gab!

Thou my soul, Thou my heart, Thou my joy, oh Thou my pain, Thou my world in which I live; Thou my Heaven, where in I soar; so Thou my grave, in which I bury my grief forever.

186. Symphony No. 8 ("Unfinished")
I, m. 94

Allegro moderato

Schubert

187. Sonata, op. 118ᶜ, Puppenwiegenlied
III, m. 9

Nicht schnell

Schumann

188. Quintet ("Die Forelle"), op. 114, D. 667

III, m. 93

Schubert

Beethoven

190. Trio, op. 11
Var. IV

*May be performed with either violin or clarinet.

191

191. Rigoletto, Act II, no. 7
m. 194

In heaven, close to God, a protective angel watches. Ah, watch over this flower.

192. Suite XVI

Courante

Handel

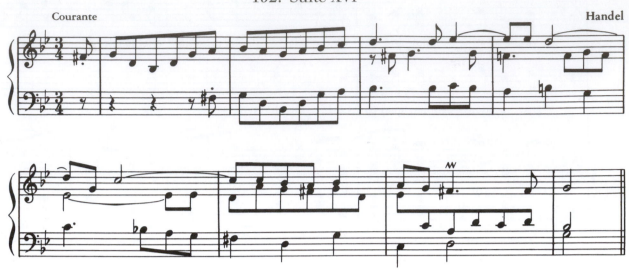

193. Sonata, op. 53
I, m. 34

Allegro con brio

Beethoven

Track 32

194. Symphony in C major ("The Great")
II, m. 93

Andante con moto

Schubert

195. Trio, op. 1, no. 3
II, Var. V, m. 19

Beethoven

196. Mass in E♭ major: Benedictus

9

Blessed is he who cometh in the name of the Lord.

----

197. Midsummer Night's Dream, op. 61: Wedding March

Allegro vivace   Mendelssohn

198. Rigoletto, Act II, no. 14
m. 64

Pardon will come to us from Heaven. This clown knows how to strike you down.

199. Christmas Oratorio, no. 4: Introduction

200. Sonata VII for Flute and Continuo
II

201. Mazurka, op. 67, no. 2
m. 17

Track 33

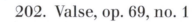

202. Valse, op. 69, no. 1

Chopin

Track 34

*See Part II, Unit 20.

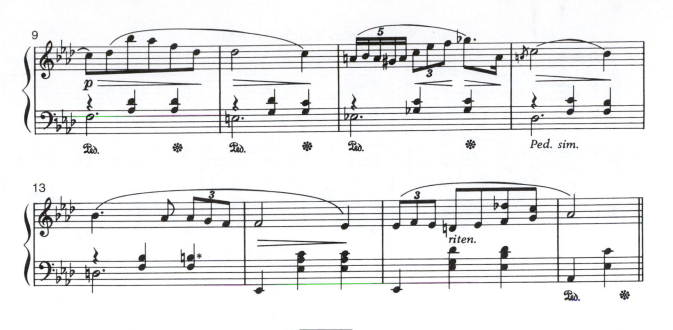

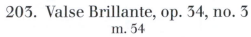

203. Valse Brillante, op. 34, no. 3
m. 54

Chopin

Track 35

*See Part II, Unit 20.

204. Someone to Watch Over Me

Gershwin

Won't you tell him please to put on some speed, Fol - low my lead,

Oh, how I need Some - one to watch o - ver

me.

205. Children's Album, op. 39, no. 1.: Morning Prayer

Tchaikovsky

Track 36

18. Modulation to Closely Related Keys

Questions for Analysis

1. Where and by what means do the modulations occur?
2. Is the new key confirmed after the point of modulation; if so, how?
3. What is the overall form of each example?

MODULATION TO DOMINANT

206. Symphony No. 39, K. 543

207. Sonata, K. 331

208. Symphony No. 2, op. 36
III

Beethoven

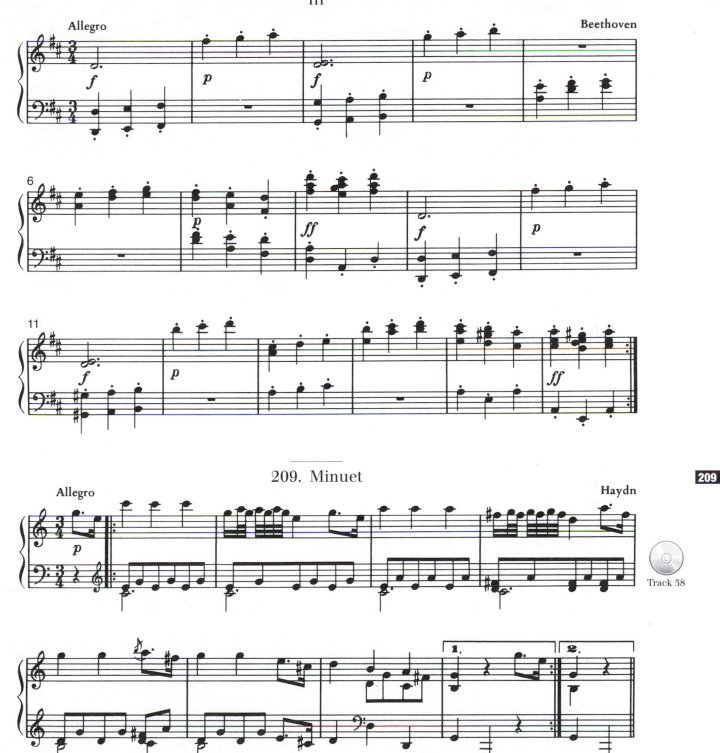

209. Minuet

Haydn

Track 38

210. Quartet, D. 173
IV

Allegro

Schubert

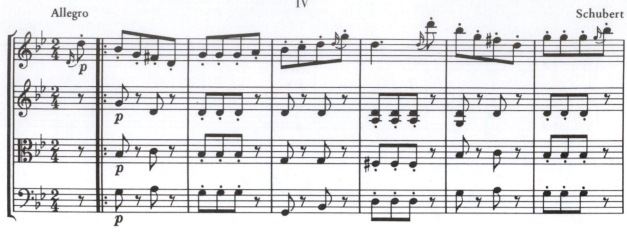

211. Sonata in C# minor, Hob. XVI: 36
II

Allegro con brio

Haydn

Track 39

146   PART II. CHROMATIC MATERIALS

212. Symphony No. 41, K. 551

III

Mozart

213. Mazurka, op. 7, no. 2

Chopin

Vivo, ma non troppo

Track 40

214. Sonata in G major, Hob. XVI: 39
III

Haydn

Allegro

Track 41

215. Sonata, K. 282, Menuet I

Mozart

Track 42

216. Quartet, D. 173
II

Andantino

Schubert

217. Trio in F♯ minor, Hob. XV: 26
II

Haydn

218. Sonata in E minor, Hob. XVI: 34
III

Molto vivace

Haydn

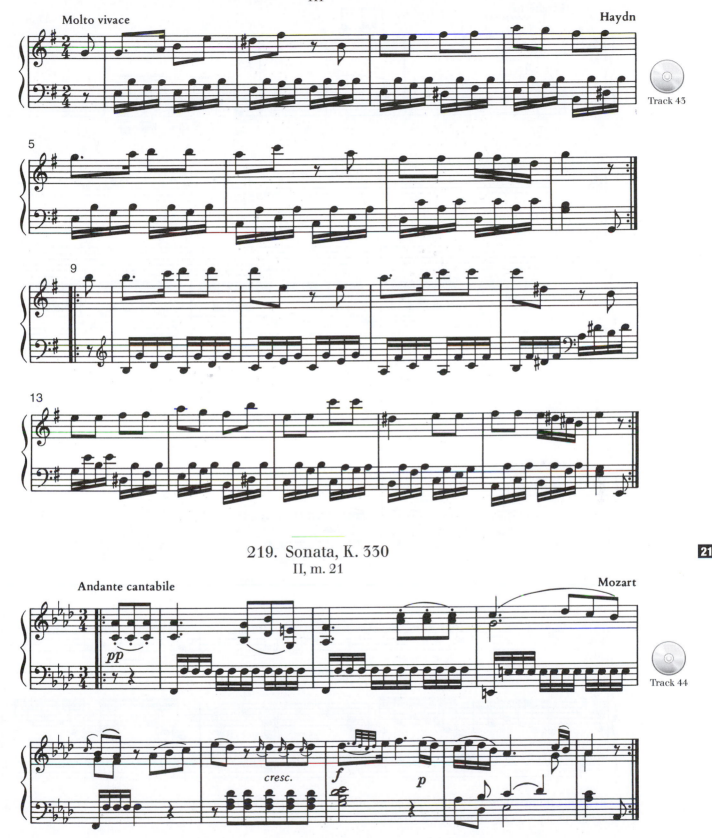

Track 43

219. Sonata, K. 330
II, m. 21

Andante cantabile

Mozart

Track 44

220. Lucia di Lammermoor, Act I, Cavatina

Reigning in the silence was the darkening night. The forehead was struck by a pallid ray of the gloomy moon.

221. Quintet, op. 115

Brahms

222. Symphony No. 7, op. 92

Beethoven

223. Symphony No. 104, Hob. I: 104

Haydn

224. Sonatina, Hob. XVI: 1
II, m. 21

Haydn

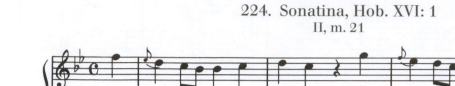

Track 45

225. Deh più a me non vàscondete

Bononcini

Con sve - lar - vi, se voi

sie - te, voi po - te - te far que - st'al - ma fuor di duol, voi po -

te - te far que-st'al-ma — fuor di duol, _____ far que-st'al-ma — fuor di _ duol.

By unveiling yourselves (if you are about to do that) you can take this soul out
of pain.

---

226. Carneval des Animaux: Le Cygne

Saint-Saëns

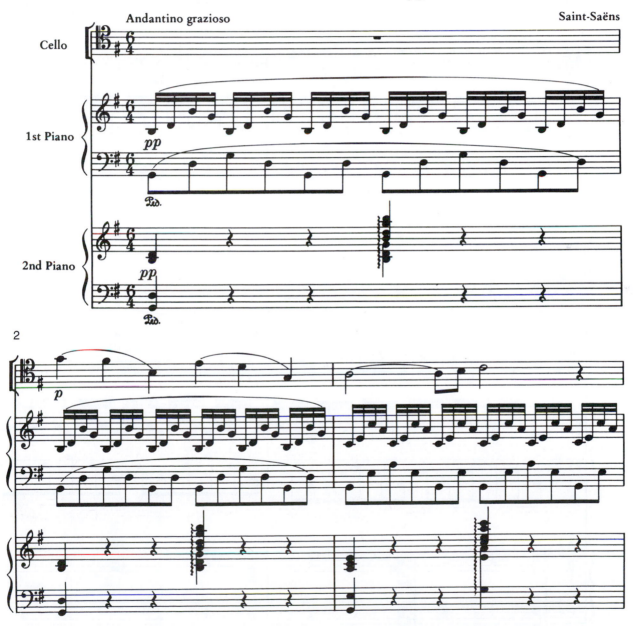

PART II. CHROMATIC MATERIALS

227. Waltz, op. 39, no. 15

Brahms

Track 46

228. Quartet, op. 18, no. 2
IV

Allegro molto quasi presto

Beethoven

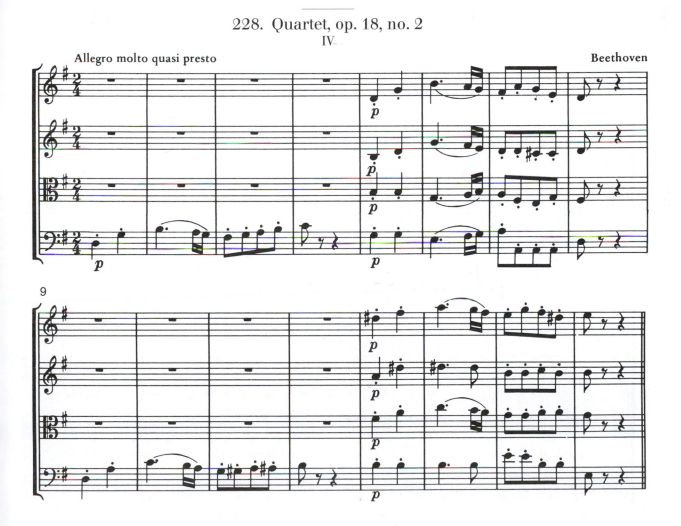

229. Dido and Aeneas, Act I, scene I
Reh. 4, m. 19

Purcell

230. French Suite in C minor

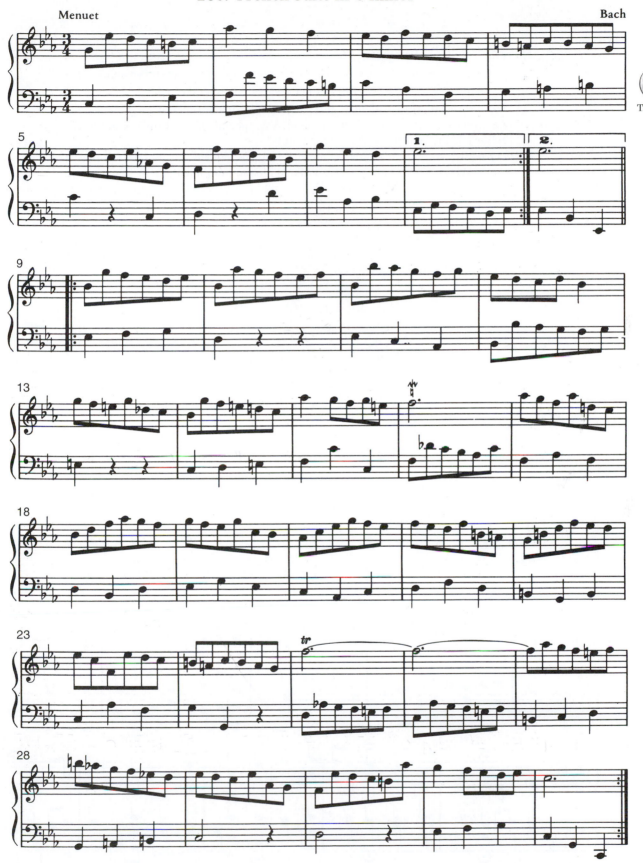

19. Complete Pieces for Analysis II

Checklist for Analysis

✓ *Subjective aspects, including affect, mood, expression:* How are these achieved?

✓ *Stylistic aspects:* What features of the music tell us who wrote it?

✓ *Form:* Overall form, cadences, phases, periodic structure if any.

✓ *Rhythm:* Meter, rhythmic patterns (motives), special effects. How is continuity achieved, and where are the resting points?

✓ *Harmony:* Harmonic details, including cadences, chords, inversions, nonharmonic tones. Which are the structural chords? Which are embellishing or linear?

✓ *Line:* Structural pitches, motives, cadence figures; placement of climax, if any.

✓ *Counterpoint and voice-leading:* How do the outer voices relate to each other in terms of intervals, intervallic patterns, relative motion, and so on? Are all tendency tones conventionally resolved?

✓ *All aspects of pattern:* Accompaniment patterns, harmonic and motivic patterns; patterns of nonharmonic tones.

231. Wachet auf, ruft uns die Stimme

Bach

Track 48

232. In dulci jubilo

Bach

Track 49

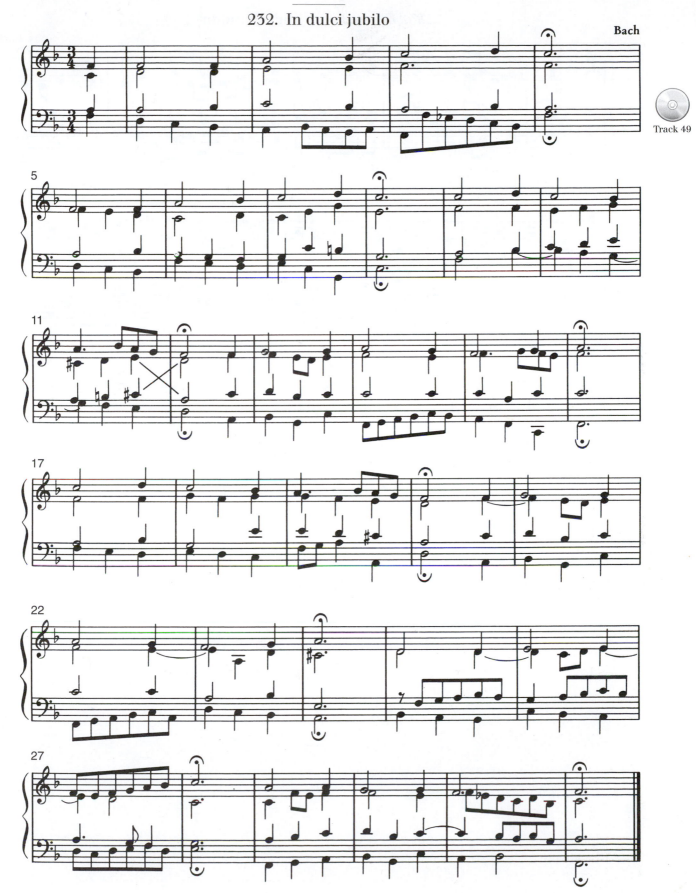

233. Christ lag in Todesbanden

Bach

234. Menuet

Handel

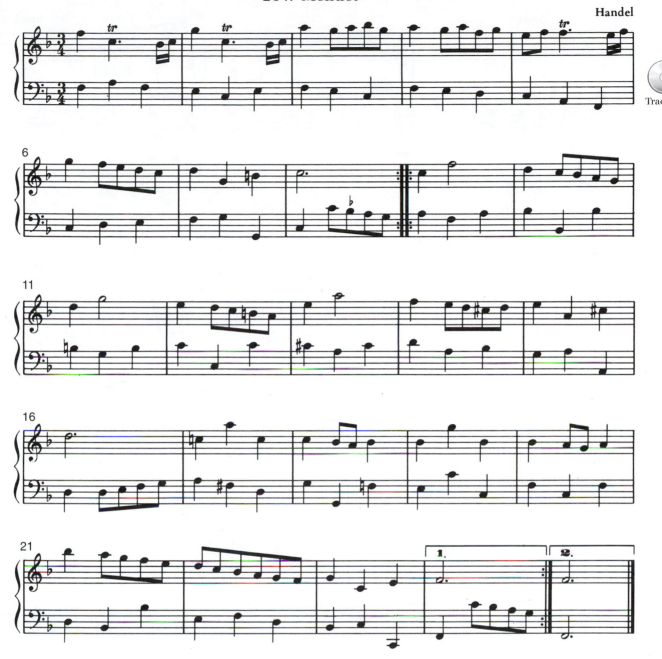

Track 50

236. Sonata, op. 118^b, Abendlied

237. Waltz, op. 39

Brahms

Poco sostenuto

Track 52

238. Prelude

239. Sonatina in F major

Allegro assai

Beethoven

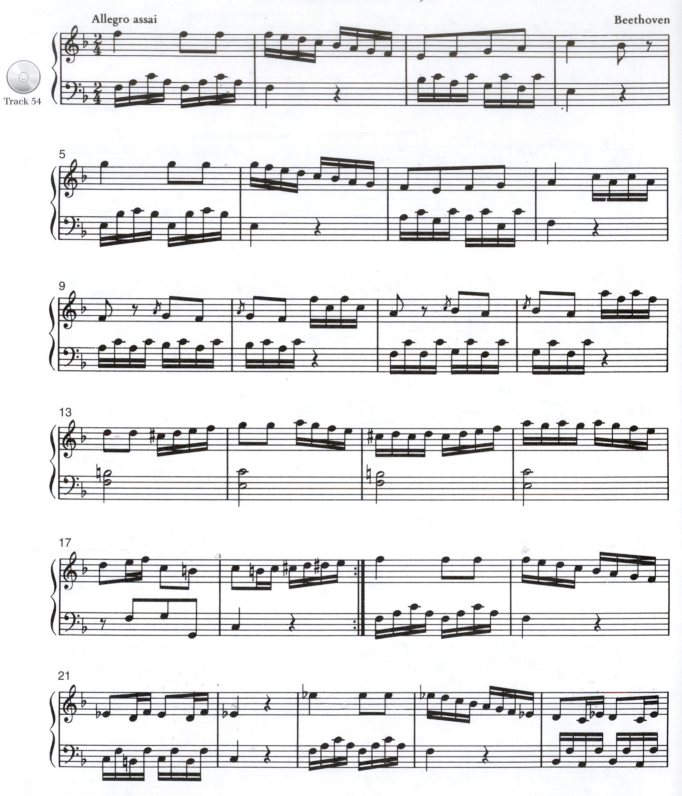

Track 54

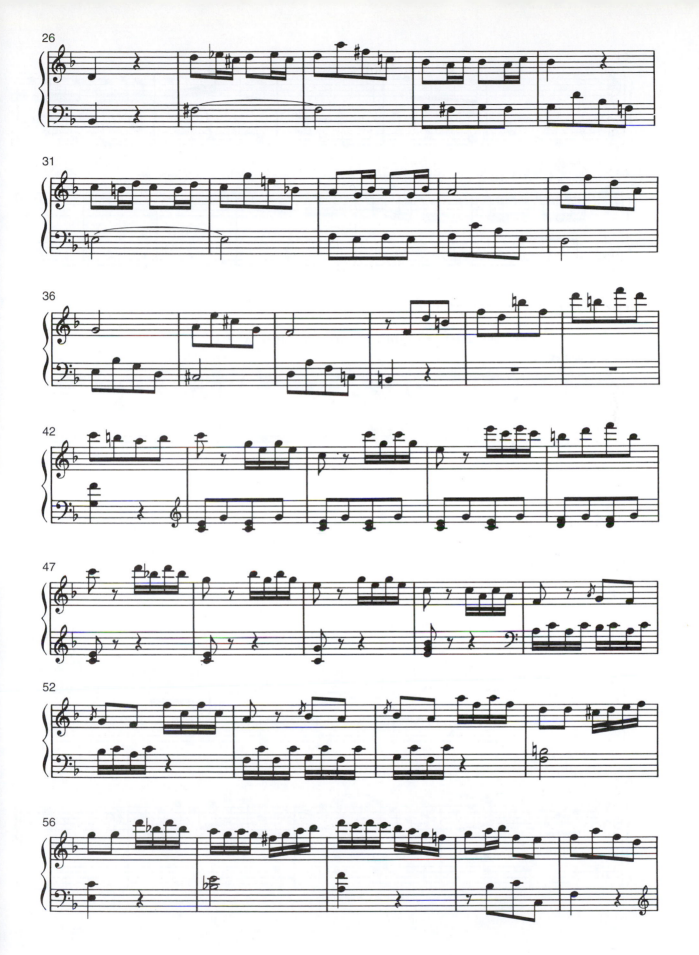

240. Sonata in G major, Hob. XVI: 27

Haydn

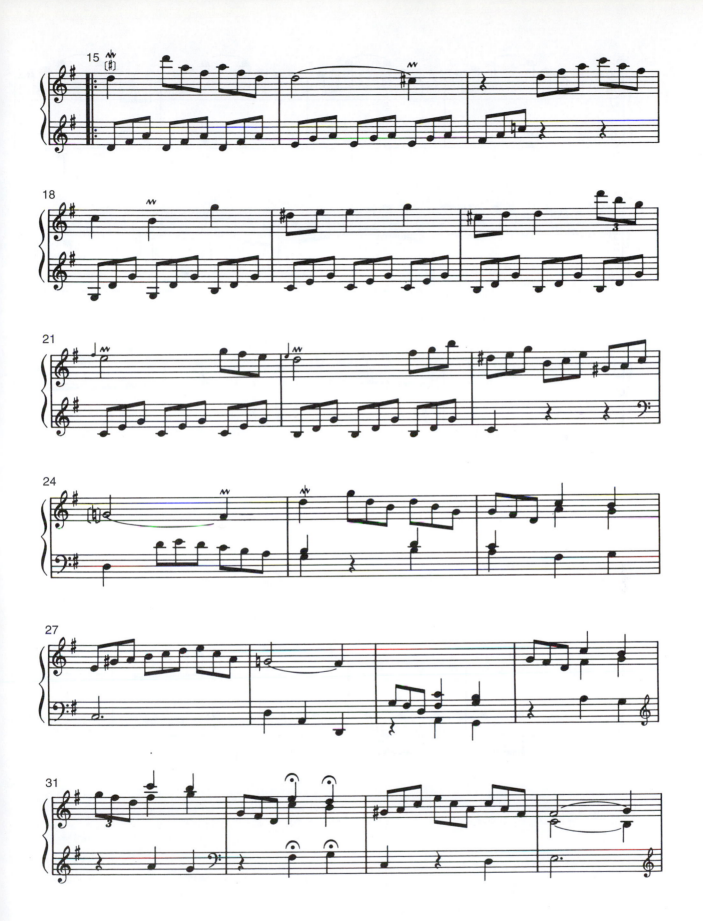

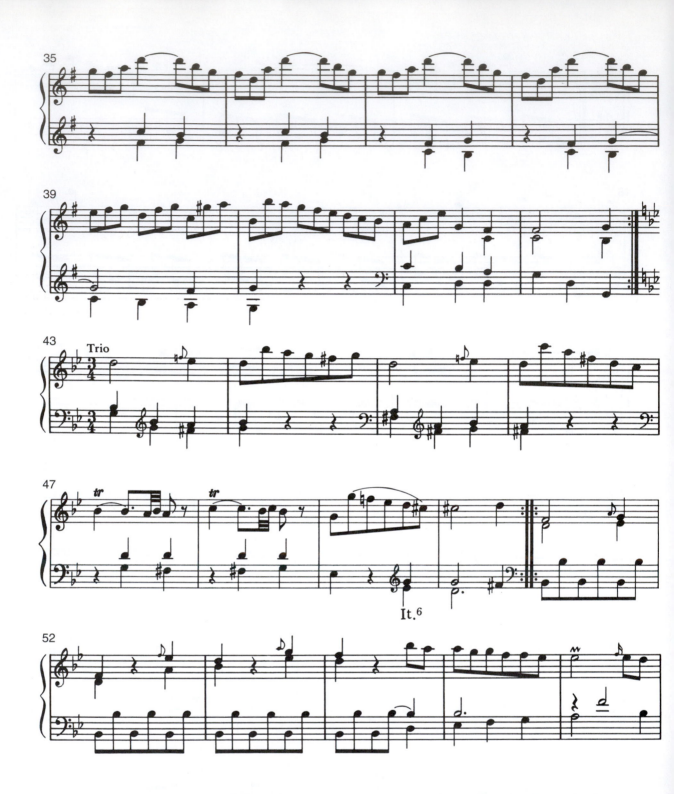

Menuet da Capo

241. I Got Rhythm

Gershwin

Refrain (with abandon)

I ___ got rhy - thm, ___ I ___ got mu - sic, ___
I ___ got my man ___ Who could ask for an - y - thing more?
I ___ got dais - ies ___ In ___ green pas - tures, ___ I ___ got
my man ___ Who could ask for an - y - thing more? Old ___ Man

* See Unit 30

* See Unit 24

** See Unit 30

20. Linear (Embellishing) Diminished Seventh Chords

Questions for Analysis

1. Which chords are clearly functional? Which are linear?
2. What combinations of nonharmonic tones create the linear chords?

242. Symphony No. 104, Hob. I: 104, Menuet

243. Symphony No. 7, op. 92
III, m. 149

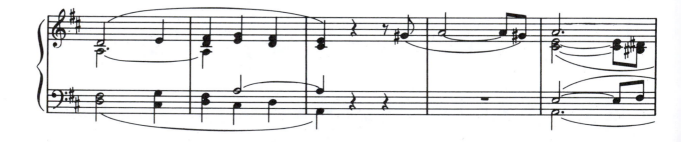

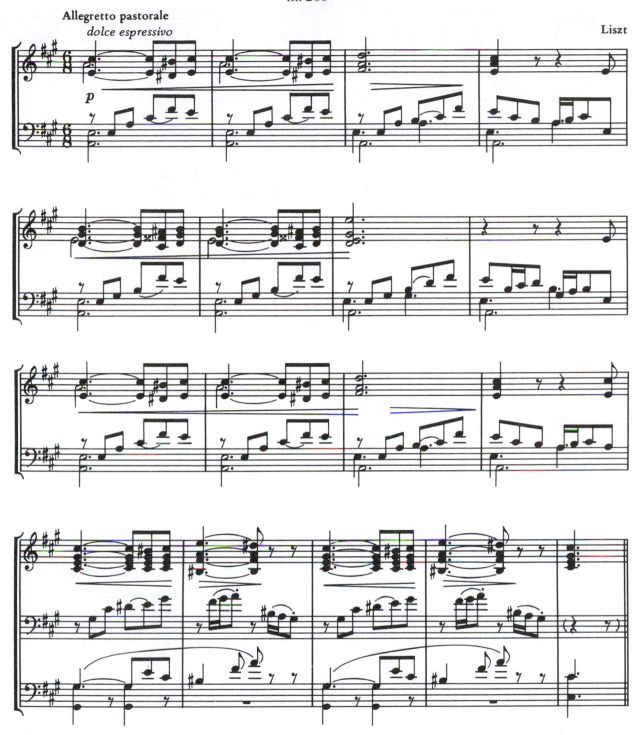

244. Les Préludes
m. 260

Allegretto pastorale
dolce espressivo

Liszt

245. Contradanse

Beethoven

Track 55

246. Symphony No. 6, op. 74
I, m. 90

Tchaikovsky

Andante

247. Quartet, op. 18, no. 3
II

Andante con moto

Beethoven

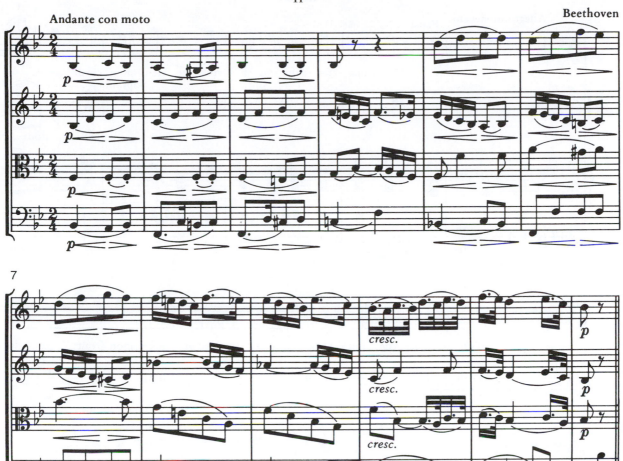

7

248. Sonata, op. 53
II

Con moto

Schubert

20. LINEAR (EMBELLISHING) DIMINISHED SEVENTH CHORDS   183

249. Faust, Act IV, no. 18
m. 204

Gounod

Faust: Sweet nectar, let my heart be enshrouded in your rapture, while a kiss of fire caresses my pale brow until daybreak.

250. Carnaval, op. 9: Arlequin
m. 17

251. Waltz, K. 567

252. Rienzi: Overture

Wagner

253. I Puritani, Act II, scene 3
Reh. 24, m. 23

Bellini

Qui la vo - ce sua so - a - ve mi chia-

ma - va e poi spa - rì. ___ Qui giu - ra - va es - ser fe-

stent.

in tempo con espress.

de - le,   qui il giu - ra - va, qui il giu - ra - va, e poi cru-

de - le,   poi cru - de - le ei mi fug - gi.

Here his sweet voice was calling for me and then it disappeared. Here he was
swearing to be faithful, and then the cruel one escaped from me.

254. Symphony No. 104, Hob. I: 104
II

Haydn

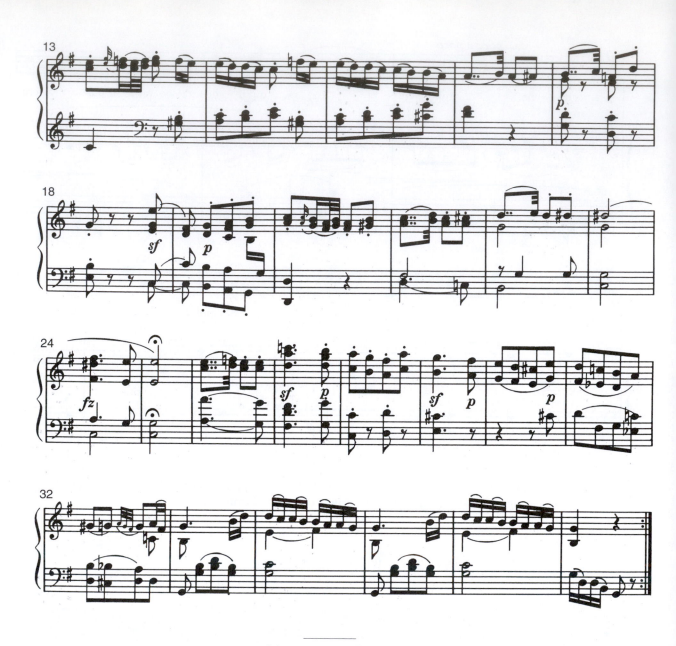

255. The Girl Friend

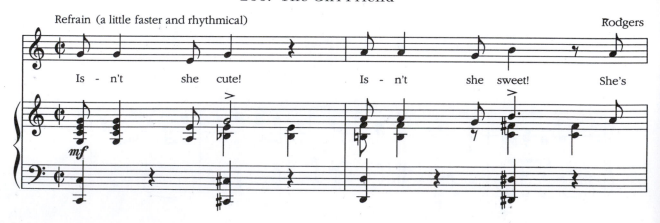

Rodgers

Refrain (a little faster and rhythmical)

Is - n't she cute! Is - n't she sweet! She's

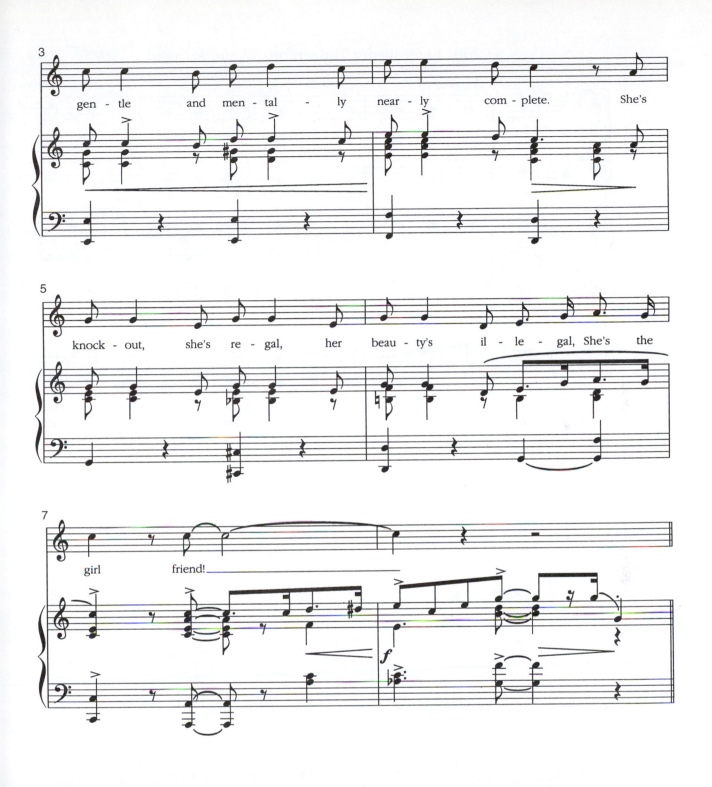

256. Liebeslieder Walzer, op. 52, no. 4

Brahms

Wie des A - bends schö - ne Rö - te
möcht' ich ar - me Dir - ne glüh'n, glüh'n,

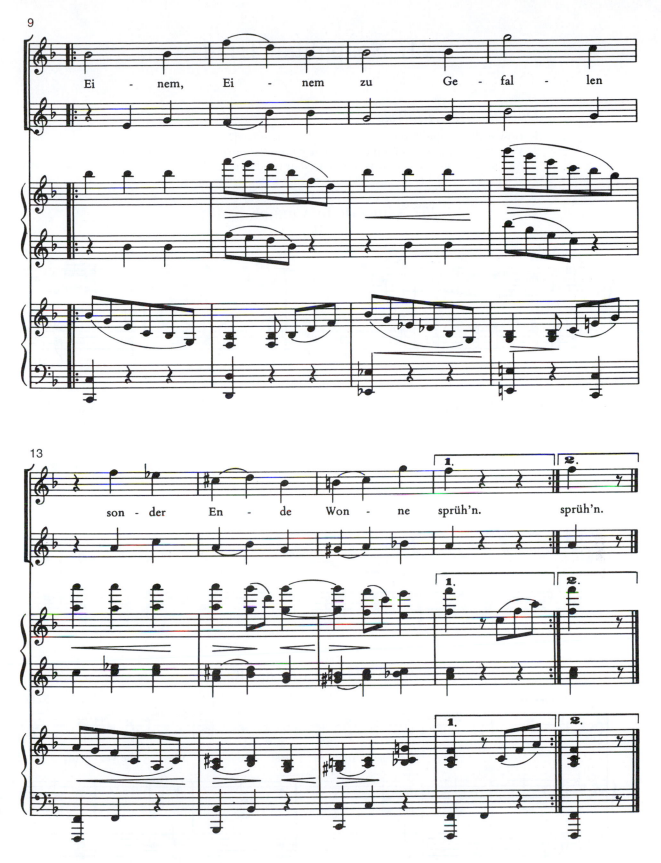

I wish to glow to you like the beautiful red of the evening, to please one person, to spread delight without end.

21. Neapolitan Triad

Questions for Analysis

1. How is the Neapolitan triad introduced and resolved?
2. Where does the Neapolitan triad occur within the phrase? Is the chord in root position or inversion? Is it tonicized or used in a modulation?

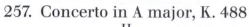

257. Concerto in A major, K. 488
II

Andante

Mozart

Track 58

5

9

258. Der Müller und der Bach

Moderato

Der Müller

Schubert

Wo ein treu - es Her - ze in Lie - be ver - geht, da

p

257

258

Where a true heart pines away for love, there droop the lilies on every bank.
Clouds conceal the moon so that men may not see her tears. Angels close their
eyes, and cry and sing the soul to rest.

259. Ach Gott, vom Himmel sieh' darein

Bach

Track 59

260. Invention No. 13
m. 18

Bach

Track 60

261. Il Trovatore, Act II, no. 8
m. 35

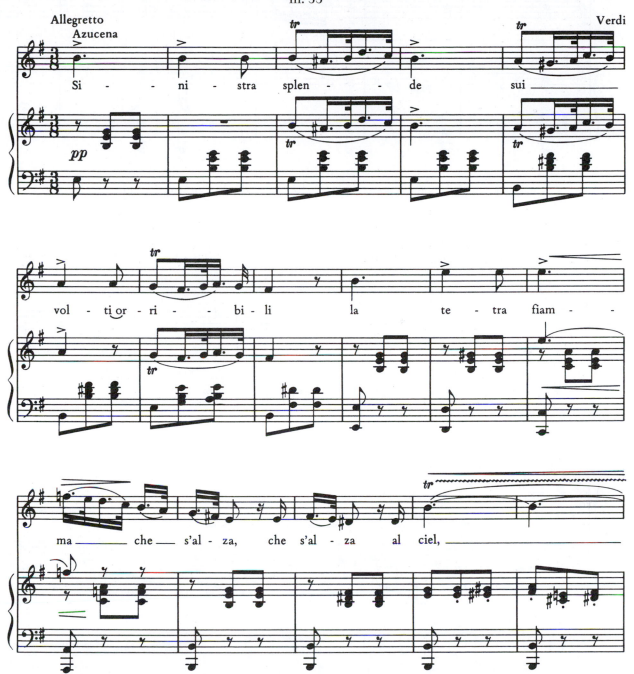

che — s'al za al ciel!

Sinister shines on the terrible faces the gloomy flame that rises to the sky.

262. Intermezzo in A major, op. 118, no. 2
m. 65

Andante teneramente

Track 61

Brahms

263. Prelude, op. 28, no. 20

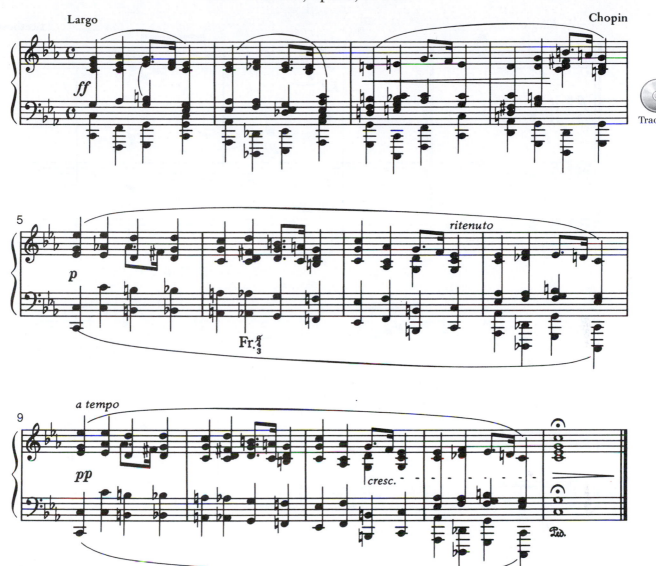

Largo

Chopin

ff

Track 62

5

p

Fr.$^{6}_{3}$

ritenuto

9

a tempo

pp

cresc.

Ped.

264. String Quartet, op. 59, no. 2

I

Beethoven

265. Wie Melodien zieht es mir, op. 105

Zart · Brahms

Wie Me - lo - di - en ____ zieht es mir lei - se durch den

Sinn, wie Früh - lings-blu - men blüht es und schwebt wie Duft da - hin.

As melodies drift lightly through my senses, as spring flowers bloom and their
fragrance floats away.

266. Quartet, op. 18, no. 3
III

Allegro · Beethoven

267. Mass in E♭ major: Credo

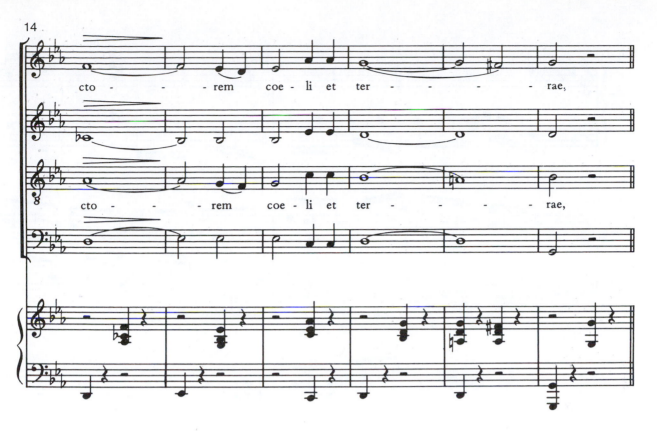

I believe in one God, maker of heaven and earth.

268. The Well-Tempered Clavier, Vol. II, Fugue 17
m. 41

Bach

———

269. Prelude, op. 28, no. 6

Chopin

Track 63

22. Augmented Sixth Chords, Submediant Degree as Lowest Note

Model Analysis **Beethoven**, *Thirty two Variations on an Original Theme*

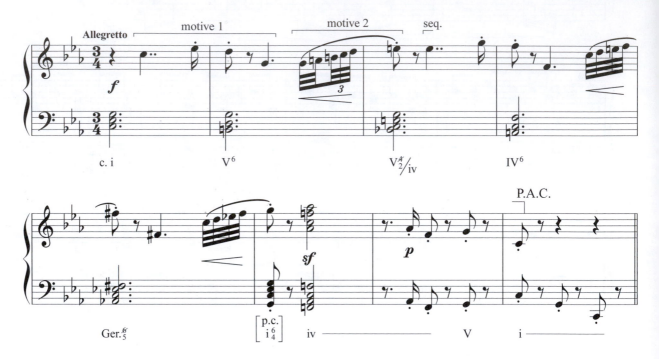

Observations:

A. Form: one phrase, ending in a perfect authentic cadence

B. The underlying stuctural harmony is i-V-i.

C. The linear/contrapuntal structure is very typical for tonal music:
- the contrary motion between the outer voices, filling out the $\hat{1}$ - $\hat{5}$ space by step, the upper voice upward and the bass downward;
- the bass line moving down chromatically, outlining the tonic-to-dominant tetrachord (perfect fourth);
- the harmonization of the bass line, which is also highly typical for tonal music; note the harmonic choices and inversions which result from the bass line.

D. Outer-Voice Structure (octave displacements simplified slightly).

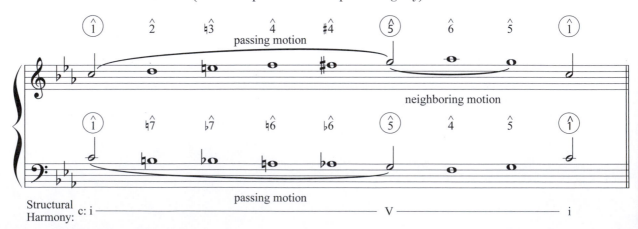

E. See also Appendix A, page 549.

Questions for Analysis

1. Where do augmented sixth chords occur?
2. How are these chords introduced and resolved?
3. Where do cadences occur? How are they established?

ITALIAN

270. Ich hab' mein' Sach' Gott heimgestellt

Bach

271. Bagatelle, op. 119, no. 1

m. 9

Beethoven

Track 64

272. Coriolan Overture, op. 62

Allegro con brio

Beethoven

273. Children's Album, op. 39, no. 10: Mazurka

Tchaikovsky

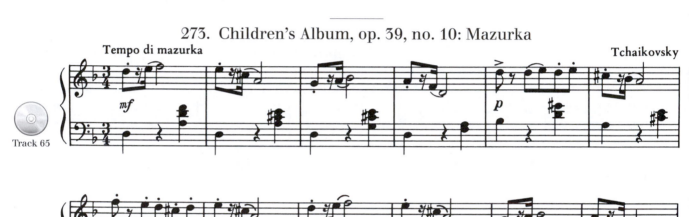

Track 65

274. Quartet, op. 168, D. 112

IV

Schubert

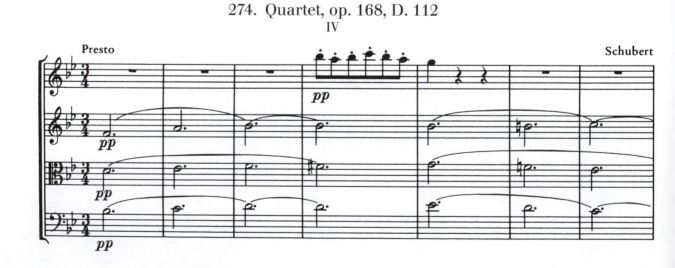

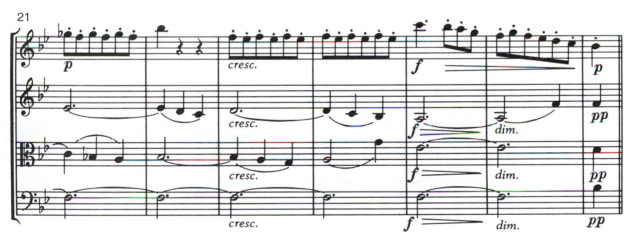

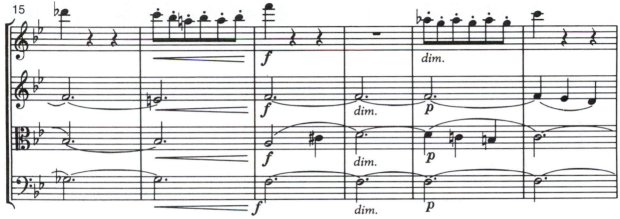

275. Symphony No. 1, op. 21
II, m. 65

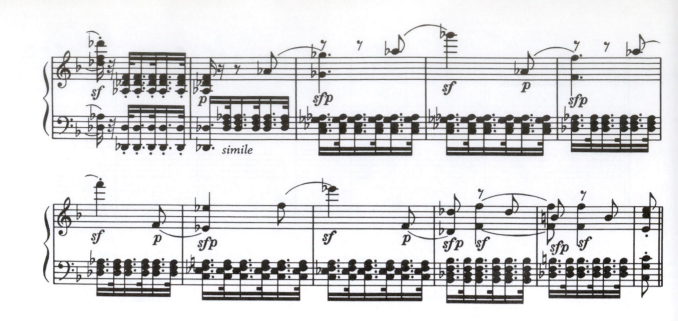

GERMAN

276. Sonata, K. 457
III, m. 167

Molto allegro

Mozart

277. Sonata, op. 109
III

Andante molto cantabile ed espressivo

mezza voce

Beethoven

Track 67

278. Trio, Hob. XV: 25

Andante

Haydn

Violin

Cello

Andante

Piano

279. **Thirty-Two Variations, WoO 80, Var. 30**

Track 68

Beethoven

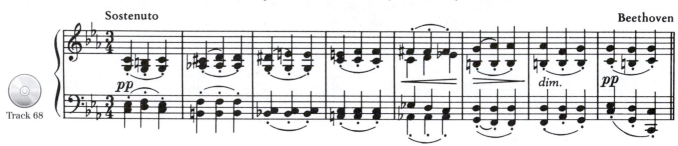

280. **Chanson Sans Paroles, op. 40, no. 2**

Sibelius

281. Der Rosenkavalier, Act I
Reh. 233

Strauss

Di ri - go - ri ar ma - to il se - no Con - tro a - mor mi ri - bel - lai, ___ Ma fui ___ vin - to in un ba - le - no ___ In ma rar du - e va - ghi rai. ___ Ma fui ___ vin - to in un ba -

le - no ahi! _____ In mi-rar du-e va - - ghi rai.

Having armed my heart with vigor against love, I rebelled. But I was defeated in a flash, alas! by looking at two delicate rays.

FRENCH

282. Elijah, op. 70, no. 1

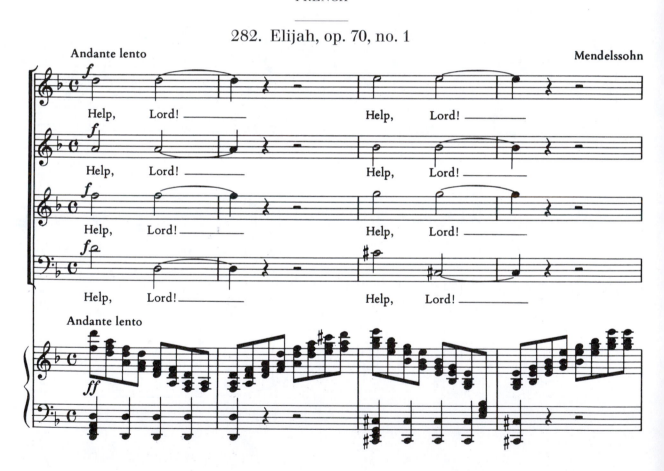

Mendelssohn

Andante lento

Help, Lord! _____ Help, Lord! _____

Help, Lord! _____ Help, Lord! _____

Help, Lord! _____ Help, Lord! _____

Help, Lord! _____ Help, Lord! _____

Andante lento

283. Mass in G major: Kyrie
m. 30

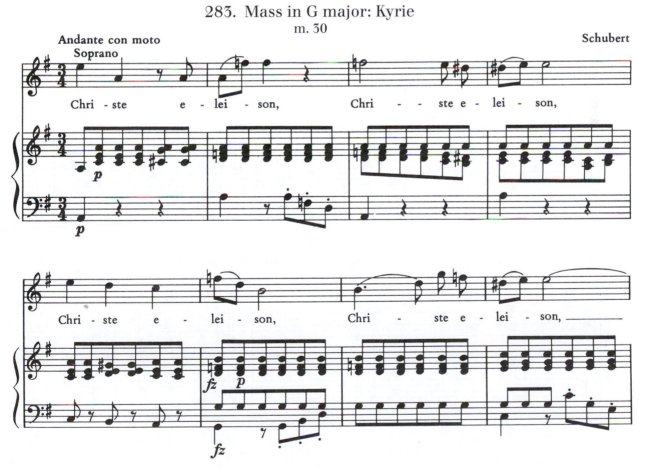

Christ, have mercy upon us.

284

284. Wer nur den lieben Gott läßt walten

Bach

285

285. Sonata, op. 42
I

Schubert

286. La Traviata, Act III: Prelude

287. Symphony in C major ("The Great")
II, m. 8

288. Alfedans, op. 12
m. 9

Grieg

Molto allegro e sempre staccato

Track 70

289. Gypsy Love Song

Herbert

Molto tranquillo

1. The birds of the for-est are call-ing for thee,_____ And the
2. The fawn that you tamed has a look in its eyes_____ That doth

shades and the glades_____ are lone-ly;_____ Sum-mer is there with her blos-soms
say: "We are too_____ long part-ed;"_____ Songs that are trolled by our com-rades

fair,_____ And you_____ are ab - sent on - ly.
old,_____ Are not now, as they were,_____ light-heart - ed.

290. Dichterliebe, op. 48, no. 12: "Am leuchtenden Sommermorgen"

On a brightening summer morning, I go into the garden. The flowers whisper and speak, but I wander silently.

23. Augmented Sixth Chords, Other Scale Degrees as Lowest Note

Questions for Analysis
1. How are the augmented sixth chords introduced and resolved?
2. Where do cadences occur? How are they established?

---

291. Adagio

Mozart (?)

Track 71

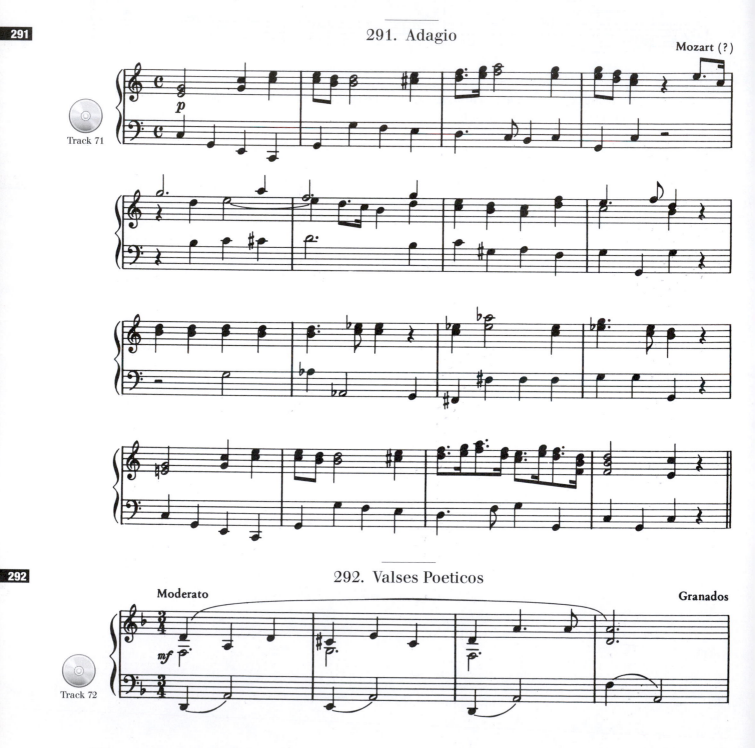

---

292. Valses Poeticos

Granados

Track 72

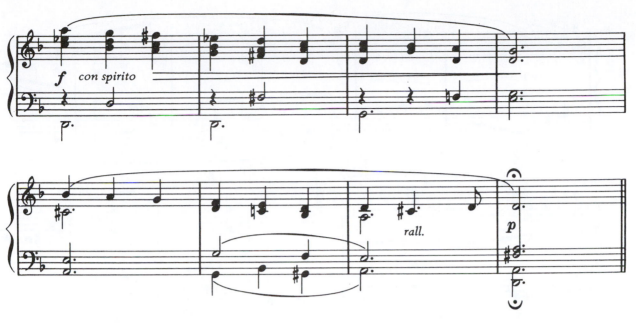

293. Symphony No. 8 ("Unfinished")
II

Schubert

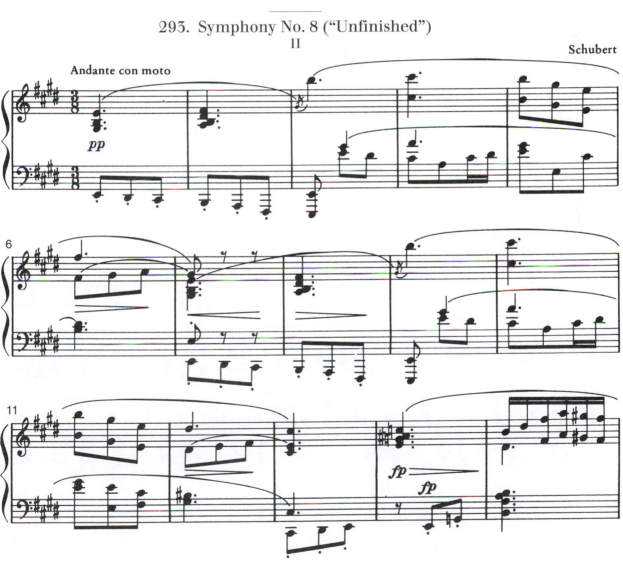

---

294. Songs and Dances of Death, no. 4

Moussorgsky

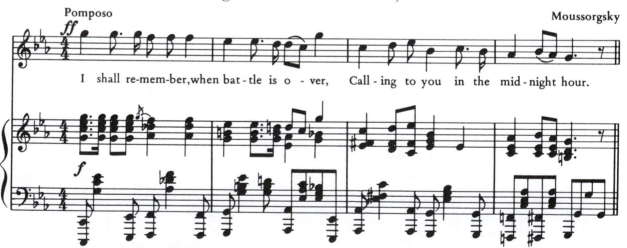

I shall re-mem-ber, when bat-tle is o-ver, Call-ing to you in the mid-night hour.

295. Orphée, Act I, nos. 6 and 7

Gluck

Object of my love . . .

24. Augmented Sixth Chords, Other Uses

Question for Analysis

1. How do the arrangement of the chord and the voice-leading serve to establish the particular usage of the chord?

LINEAR

296. Rigoletto, Act I: Prelude

Verdi

297. Song Without Words, op, 40, no. 6

Tchaikovsky

Track 73

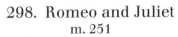

298. Romeo and Juliet
m. 251

Tchaikovsky

Allegro giusto

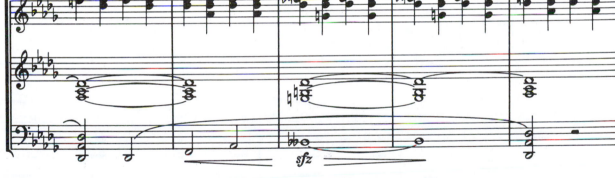

299. Waltz

Schubert

Track 74

300. Intermezzo, op. 76, no. 4

Brahms

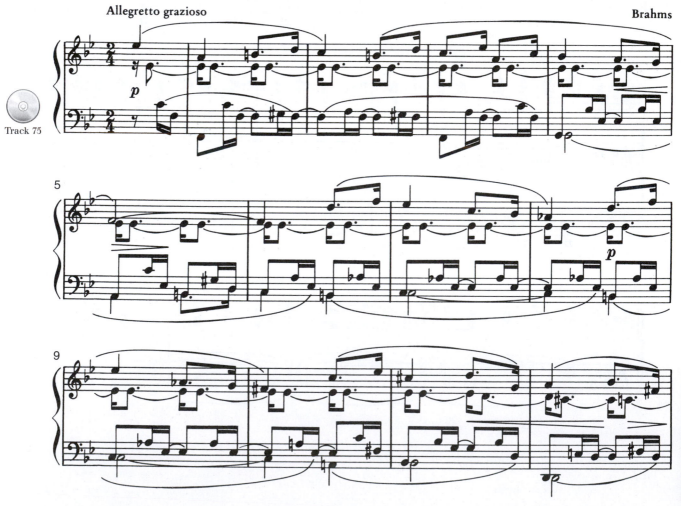

301. Children's Album, op. 39, no. 20: The Witch (Baba Yaga)

302. Prelude, op. 28, no. 22

Molto agitato

Chopin

Track 77

303. Mass in G major: Benedictus

Andante grazioso

Soprano solo

Schubert

Be - ne - di - - ctus qui

Blessed is he who cometh in the name of the Lord.

304. Die Allmacht, op. 79, no. 2

Schubert

Great is Jehovah the Lord, for heaven and earth proclaim His power.

305. Quintet, op. 163
IV, m. 417

Schubert

306. Liebestraum, no. 3

Liszt

Poco allegro, con affetto

307. Snowmaiden: Chanson du Bonhomme Hiver

Rimsky-Korsakov

Poco animato

308. Solvejg's Lied
m. 8

25. Other Means of Modulation

Model Analysis

Gounod: *Romeo and Juliet*

Observations:

A. Form: three-phrase sequential pattern; there is a three-measure sequence unit, transposed upward twice by minor third, for a total of three iterations.

B. Keys: The key-areas follow this transposition pattern, with music in Cb, D and F, at which point the music settles in F major.

C. Melodic line: The upper voice forms a chromatic scale upward from Ab to F.

D. Harmonic pattern: The underlying harmony forms a circle of fifths, with chord-roots progressing around the circle from Ab to F.

E. Motive: The motivic material is highly limited, with the first six beats of each sequence iteration forming the main idea, and the following six beats simply prolonging the goal harmony (and structural pitch) of each phrase.

F. See also Appendix A, page 549.

Question for Analysis

1. Identify the initial key and the key(s) to which the examples modulate. What modulatory devices are employed?

309. Mass in G major: Gloria
m. 40

Soprano: Lord God, Lamb of God.
Bass: Son of God, who taketh away the sins of the world.
Chorus: Have mercy upon us.

---

310. Wenn du nur zuweilen lächelst, op. 57, no. 2

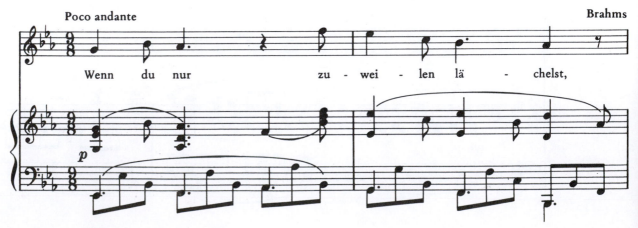

Brahms

Poco andante

Wenn du nur zu - wei - len lä - chelst,

nur — zu - wei - len Küh - le fä - chelst

die - ser un - ge-mess - nen Glut, die - ser un - ge - mess — nen Glut.

If you would only occasionally smile, or occasionally cool my boundless ardor . . .

311. Symphony No. 5, op. 67
II, m. 23

Beethoven

312. Waltz, op. 9, no. 14, D. 365
m. 17

Schubert

Track 80

313. Die Entführung aus dem Serail, K. 384, Act III, no. 18

Mozart

In Moh - ren - land ge - fan - gen war_____ ein

In Moorishland, a pretty maiden with black hair was imprisoned. She wept day and night and would gladly have been rescued.

314. Symphony No. 2, op. 61
III

315. Symphony No. 7, op. 92
II, m. 117

240   PART II. CHROMATIC MATERIALS

316. String Quartet, op. 76, no. 6
III, m. 31

Haydn

---

317. Sonata, op. 13
I, m. 132

Beethoven

Track 81

---

318. Trio, op. 70, no. 1
IV, m. 375

Beethoven

319. Prelude, op. 13, no. 3

Scriabin

Track 82

320. Die Fledermaus: Overture
Reh. 3, m. 29

J. Strauss

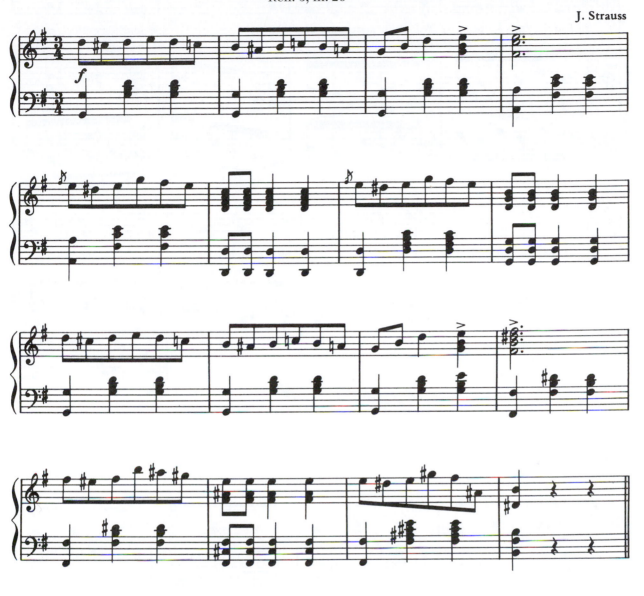

321. Wie bist du meine Königin, op. 32, no. 9
m. 39

Brahms

voll.

Through dead wastes I wander, green shadows broadening about me, endlessly
onward through the frightful oppressiveness, pleasureful . . .

322. Mass in A♭ major: Agnus Dei

Adagio

Schubert

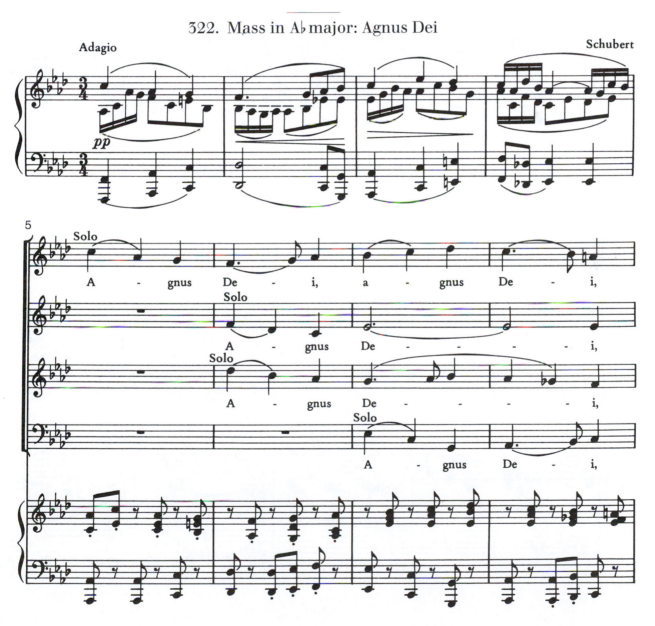

A - gnus De - i, a - gnus De - i,

A - gnus De - - - i,

A - gnus De - - - i,

A - gnus De - i,

Lamb of God, who taketh away the sins of the world, have mercy upon us.

323. Trio, op. 11
II, m. 27

Beethoven

*Violin and clarinet are alternate parts.

PART II. CHROMATIC MATERIALS

324. Melodie, op. 3, no. 3
m. 10

Rachmaninoff

325. Symphony No. 8 ("Unfinished")
II, m. 64

Schubert

26. Ninth Chords

Questions for Analysis

1. How is the ninth introduced and resolved?
2. Is it clearly heard as a chord tone, or in some cases might it better be analyzed as nonharmonic?
3. Is the chord complete or incomplete? If incomplete, which notes are missing?
4. Discuss the texture of each example.

DOMINANT NINTHS
_____

326. Artist's Life Waltzes, op. 316, no. 3
m. 17

326

J. Strauss

Track 83

_____

327. Sonata for Violin and Piano
I

327

Allegretto ben moderato

Franck

pp

328. Theme from Six Easy Variations, WoO 77

Andante, quasi Allegretto

Beethoven

Track 84

329. Valse Brillante, op. 34, no. 1
m. 128

Chopin

Track 85

330. Waldesgespräch, op. 39, no. 3

Ziemlich rasch

Schumann

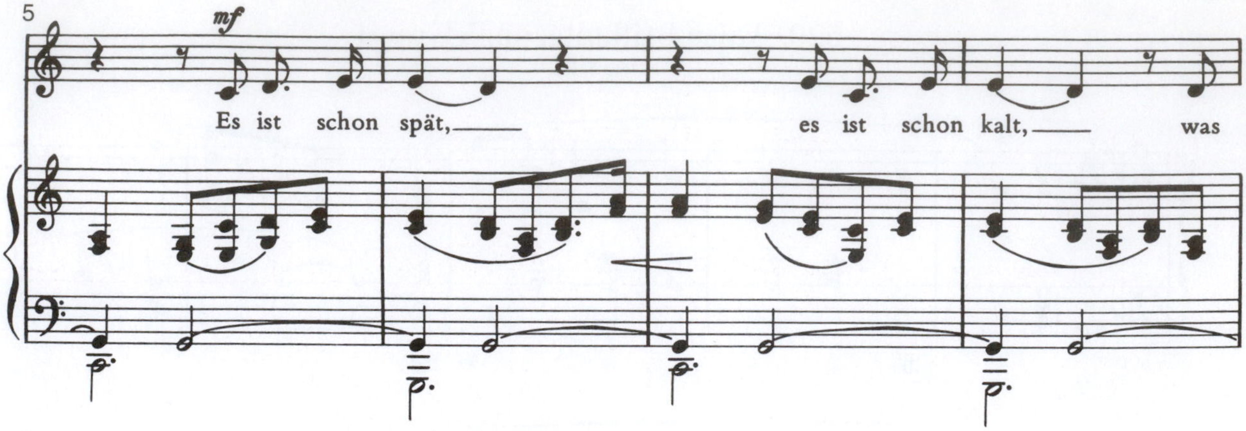
5
mf
Es ist schon spät, es ist schon kalt, was

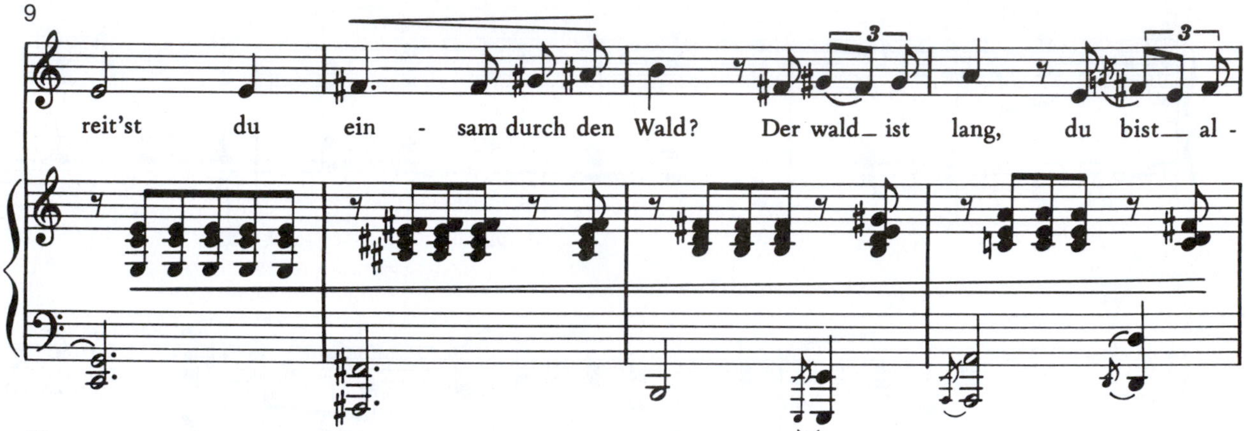
9
reit'st du ein - sam durch den Wald? Der wald ist lang, du bist al -
3

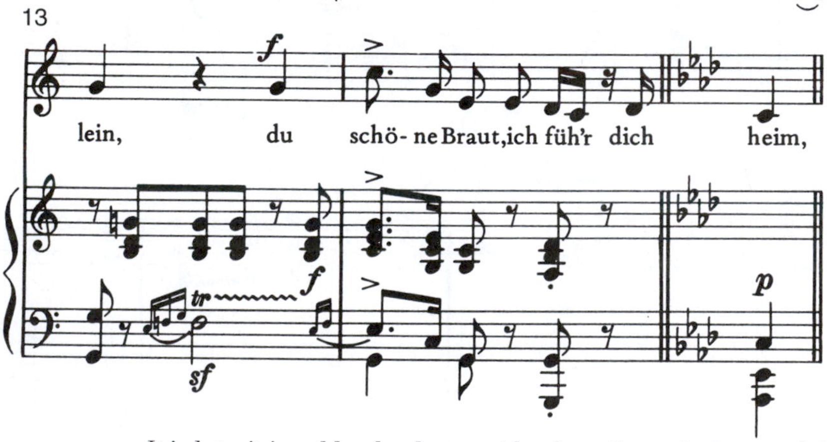
13
f
lein, du schö - ne Braut, ich füh'r dich heim,
tr
sf
p

It is late, it is cold, why do you ride alone through the woods? The way is long, you are alone–lovely bride, I will lead you home.

331. Prelude, op. 28, no. 15

Sostenuto **Chopin**

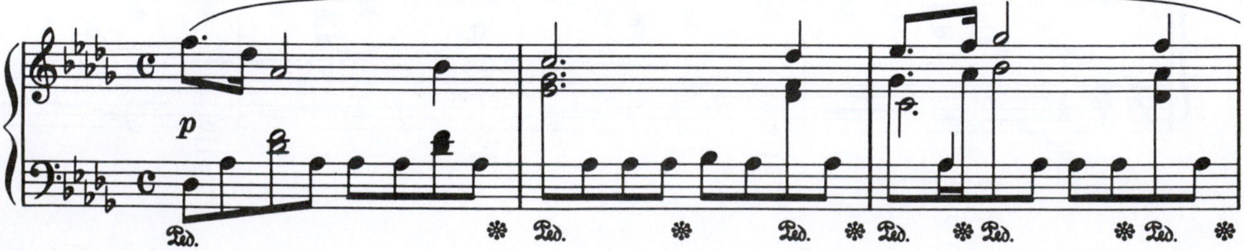
p

Track 86

332. St. Matthew Passion, no. 78

Bach

333. Genoveva, op. 81: Overture

Schumann

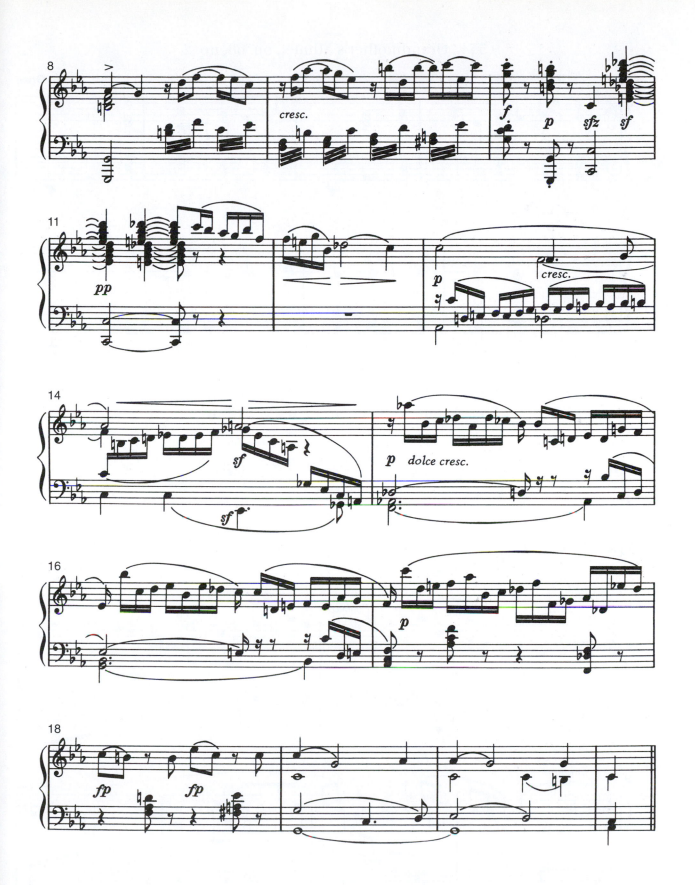

334. Grandmother's Minuet, op. 68, no. 2

Grieg

Allegretto grazioso e leggierissimo

335. Kinderszenen, op. 15, no. 7: Träumerei

Schumann

Moderato

NONDOMINANT NINTHS

336. Wedding Day at Troldhaugen, op. 65, no. 6
m. 3

Grieg

Track 89

337. Midsummer Night's Dream, op. 21: Overture
m. 450

338. Après un Rêve
m. 17

Tu m'ap - pe - lais_____ et je quit - tais la ter - - re

Pour m'en-fuir a - vec toi vers la lu - miè - - re,

Les cieux_____ pour_____ nous_____ entr' ouv - raient leurs nu - es, splen -

deurs_____ in - con - nu - es lu - eurs di - vi - nes en - tre - vu - es.

You called me and I left the earth to fly with you toward the light. The skies half opened their clouds to us, partially revealing unknown splendors, divine lights . . .

27. Extended Linear Usages

Model Analysis

Mozart, *Don Giovanni, Overture*

Observations:

A. Form: one long phrase, moving from tonic to dominant.

B. Line: the bass line forms the principal structure, a very common tonic-dominant chromatic decending line (tetrachord). The upper voice prolongs the tonic and dominant notes, moving overall from tonic to dominant.

C. Harmony: the harmonic choices are largely traditional ones, dictated by the bass line; there is only one unusual chord, a passing vi7 in m. 9; secondary diminished-seventh chords have been chosen, for their tension, and the dominant goal harmony is preceded, typically, by an augmented-sixth chord (German in this case).

D. Harmonic rhythm: the harmonic rhythm is slow at the beginning and end (harmonic prolongation), and faster in the middle section, where more harmonic and rhythmic tension is achived.

E. Counterpoint: the bass line dominates this excerpt, but note the contrary-motion arrival at the dominant in the outer voices in mm. 10-11.

F. Bass-line structure.

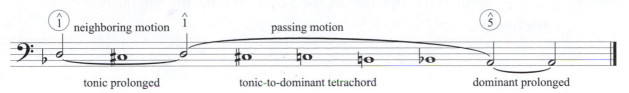

neighboring motion   passing motion

tonic prolonged   tonic-to-dominant tetrachord   dominant prolonged

G. See also Appendix A, page 549.

Questions for Analysis

1. Which chords are clearly functional and which are linear?
2. Are there chords that could be analyzed as either linear or functional?
3. How does voice-leading create linear chords?

339. Mazurka, op. 6, no. 1

Chopin

Track 90

340. "Der Tod, das ist die kühle Nacht," op. 96, no. 1

Brahms

Death, it is the cool night; life, the sultry day.
It grows dark, I become sleepy; the day has made me tired.

341. Euryanthe: Overture
m. 129

Weber

342. Variations on a Theme by Handel, var. 20

Brahms

Track 91

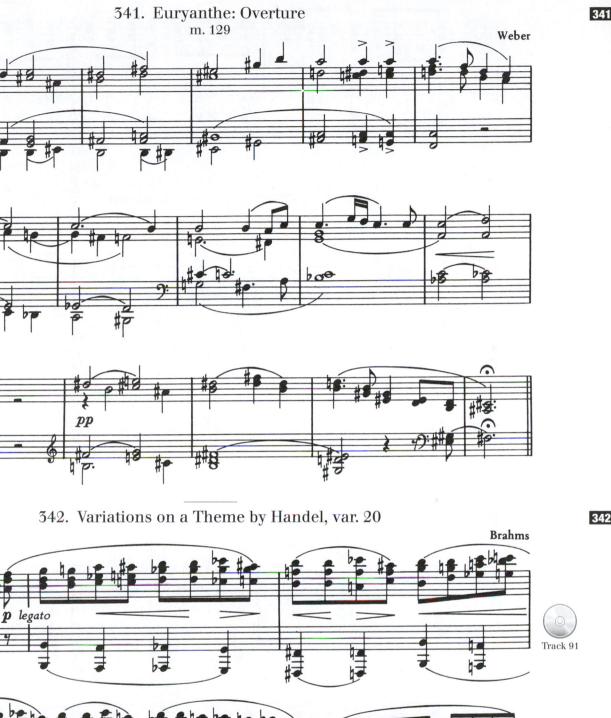

343. Symphony in D minor

III, m. 318

Allegro non troppo

Franck

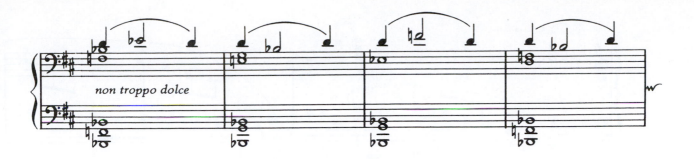

344. Lohengrin, Act I, scene 2
m. 118

Allmählich noch etwas langsamer

Wagner

345. Wotan's Farewell, Die Walküre, Act III
m. 624

Wagner

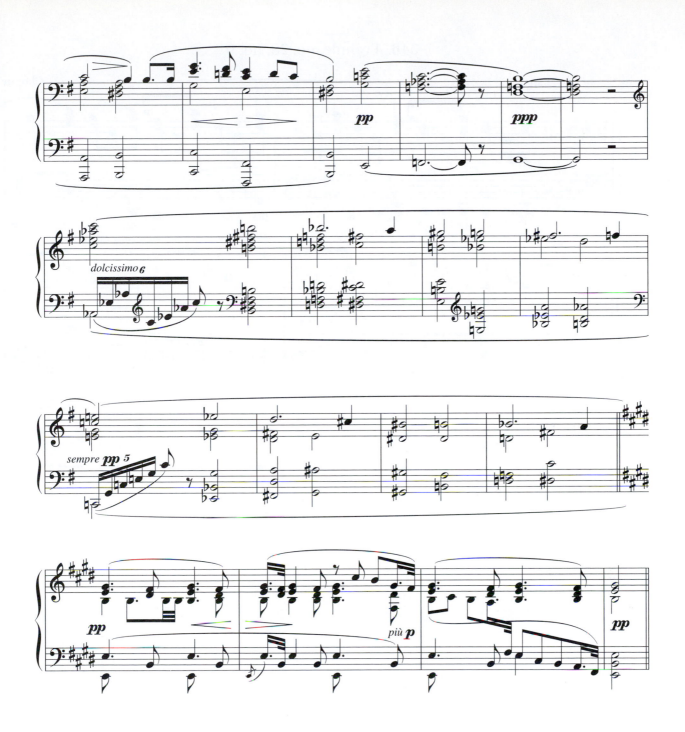

346. Prelude, op. 28, no. 9

Chopin

Track 92

347. Quartet, op. 18, no. 6

LA MALINCONIA
Questo pezzo si deve trattare colla più gran delicatezza.

Beethoven

28. Complete Pieces for Analysis III

Checklist for Analysis

✓ *Subjective aspects, including affect, mood, expression:* How are these achieved?

✓ *Stylistic aspects:* What features of the music tell us who wrote it?

✓ *Form:* Overall form, cadences, phases, periodic structure if any.

✓ *Rhythm:* Meter, rhythmic patterns (motives), special effects. How is continuity achieved, and where are the resting points?

✓ *Harmony:* Harmonic details, including cadences, chords, inversions, nonharmonic tones. Which are the structural chords? Which are embellishing or linear?

✓ *Line:* Structural pitches, motives, cadence figures; placement of climax, if any.

✓ *Counterpoint and voice-leading:* How do the outer voices relate to each other in terms of intervals, intervallic patterns, relative motion, and so on? Are all tendency tones conventionally resolved?

✓ *All aspects of pattern:* Accompaniment patterns, harmonic and motivic patterns; patterns of nonharmonic tones.

348

348. Ein' feste Burg ist unser Gott

Bach

349. Es ist genug, so nimm, Herr

Bach

350. Minuet, K. 355

Mozart

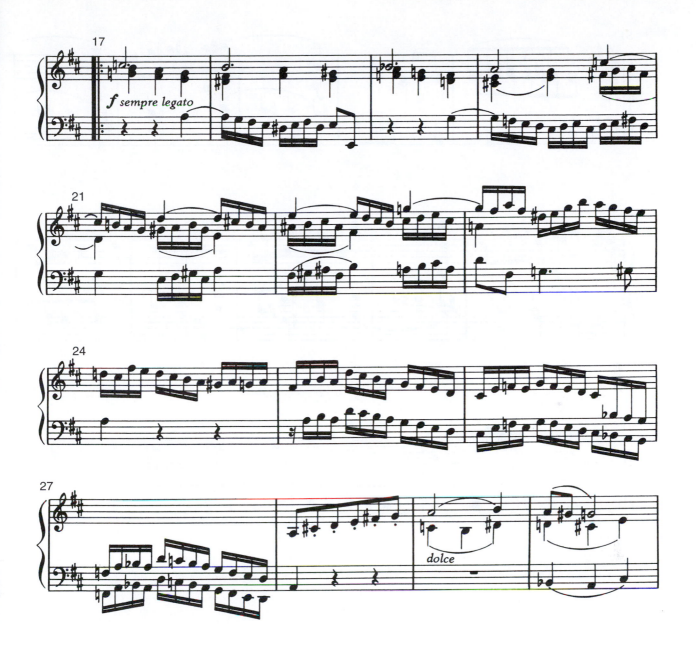

351. Myrthen, op. 25, no. 24

Schumann

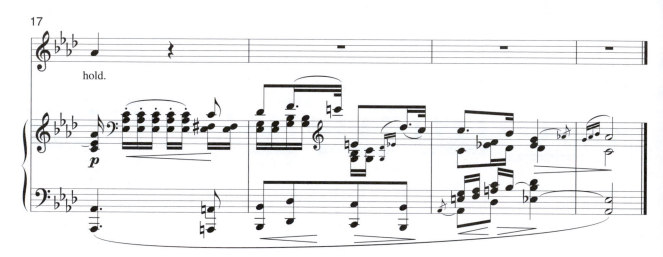

be - tend, daß Gott dich er - hal - te so rein und schön und

hold.

You are like a flower, just as charming, beautiful and pure; I look at you, and sadness steals into my heart. It seems to me I should place my hands on your head, praying that God keep you so pure, beautiful, and charming.

352. Lieder ohne Wörte, op. 30, no. 3

Mendelssohn

353. Mazurka, Op. posth. 67, no.2

Chopin

354. Phantasiestücke, op. 12, no. 3: Warum?

Schumann

355. Lyric Pieces, op. 43, no. 5: Erotikon

Grieg

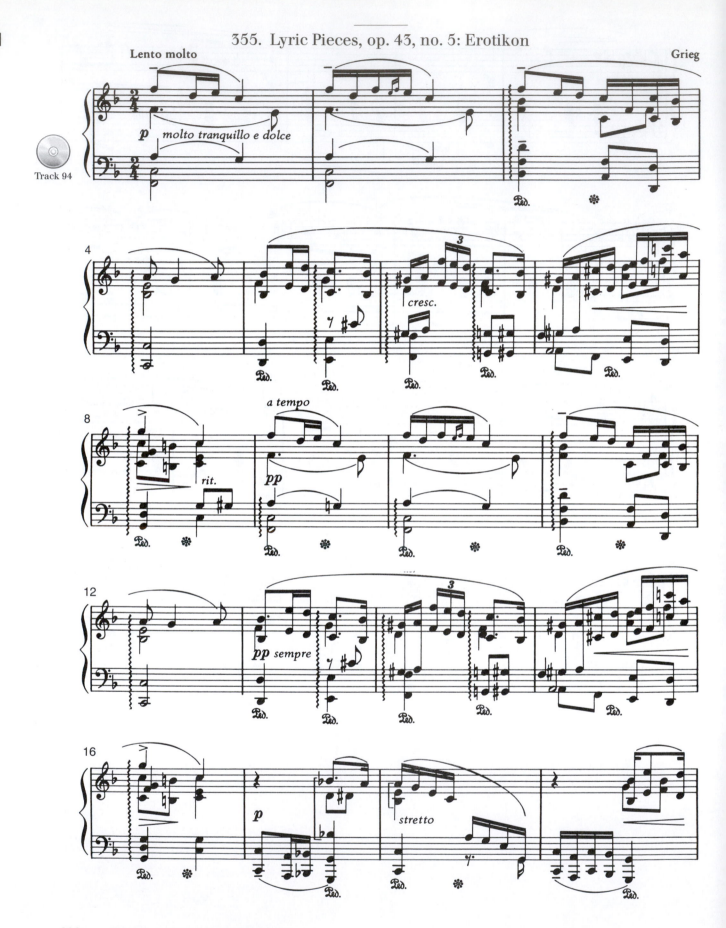

Track 94

356. Il pensieroso, from Années de Pèlerinage

Liszt

Track 95

357. Morgen, op. 27, no. 4

R. Strauss

And tomorrow the sun will shine again, and on the way where I am going, we, the happy ones, will again be one in the midst of the sun-drenched earth. And toward that far and hazy horizon, we will quietly and slowly wander. Mute, we will gaze into each other's eyes, while on us falls the blissful silence.

358. Wesendonck Lieder, no. 1: Der Engel

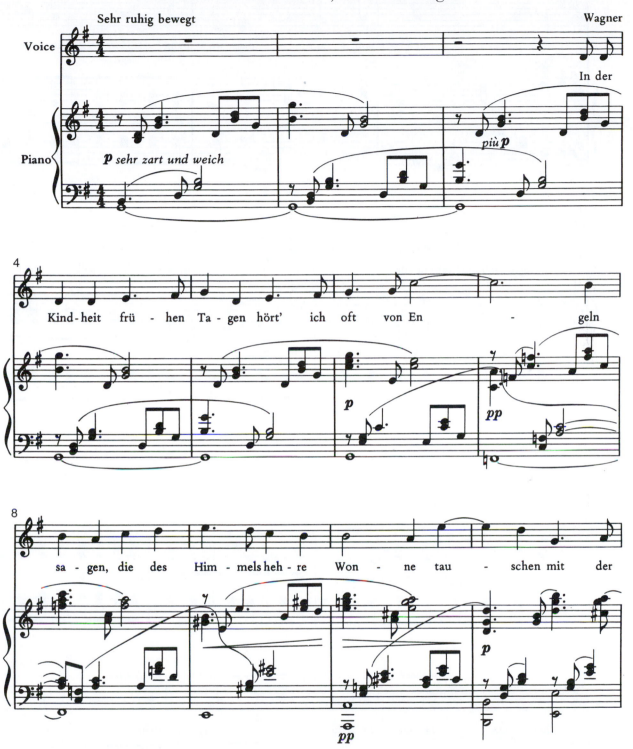

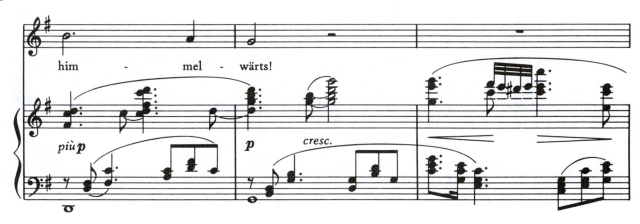

In the early days of childhood, I often heard about angels who exchange the joys of heaven for earth's sunshine; so that wherever a sorrowful heart, hidden from the world, pines; wherever it bleeds silently and fades away in tears; wherever its earnest prayer begs for release; there the angel sweeps down and gently carries it to heaven. Yes, an angel also came down to me, and on shining wings, far from all pain, bears my soul to heaven!

359. Sieben Variationen
über das Volkslied: "God Save the King", WoO 78

Beethoven

Var. V

Con espressione

sempre legato

PART II. CHROMATIC MATERIALS

360. Symphony No. 40, K. 550
III

Menuetto. Allegretto

Mozart

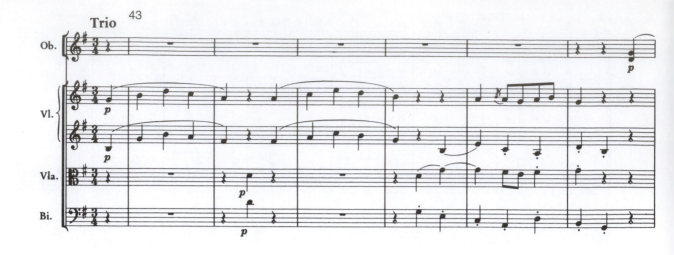

D.C. Menuetto

28. COMPLETE PIECES FOR ANALYSIS III   309

361. Phantoms, from Sketches, op. 15

Beach

362. A Breeze from Alabama: March and Two-Step

Joplin

363. Prelude, Act I, Tristan und Isolde

Einleitung

Langsam und schmachtend

Wagner

PART II. CHROMATIC MATERIALS

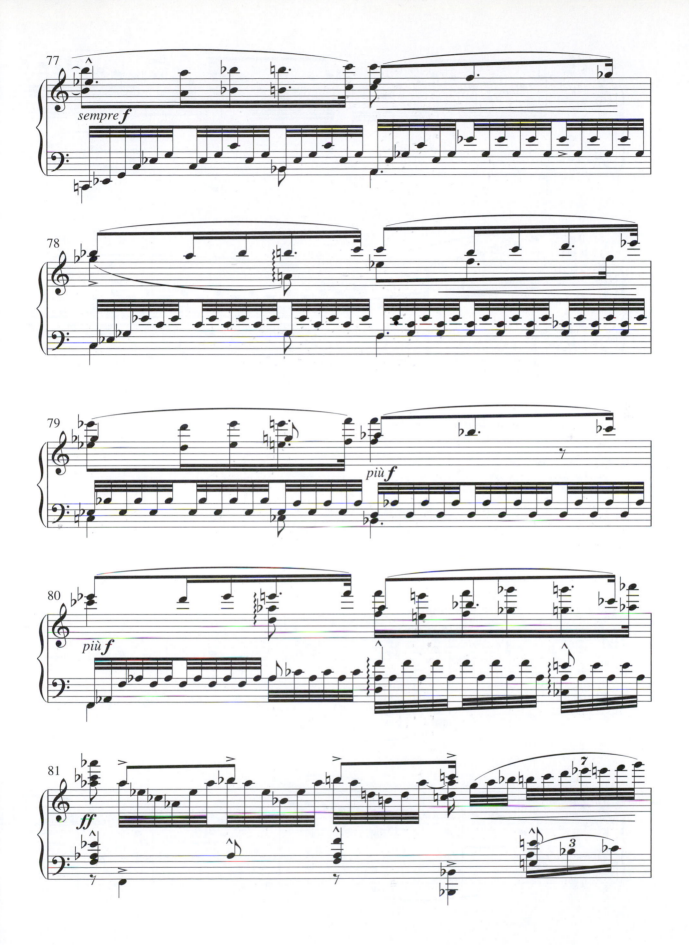

(Der Vorhang geht auf.)

364. Sonata, K. 309

Allegro con spirito

Mozart

Andante, un poco Adagio

Allegretto grazioso

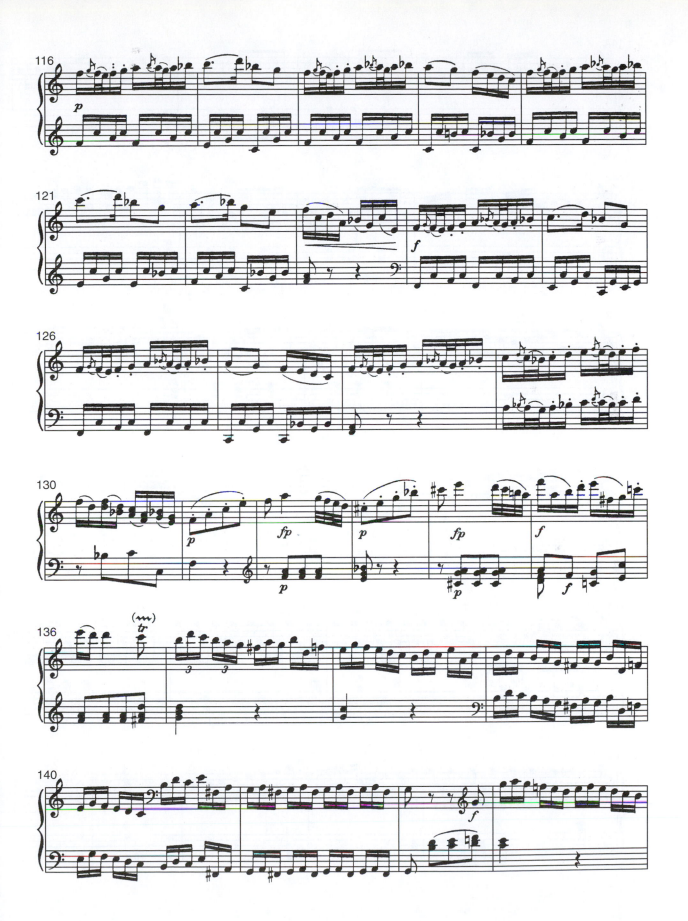

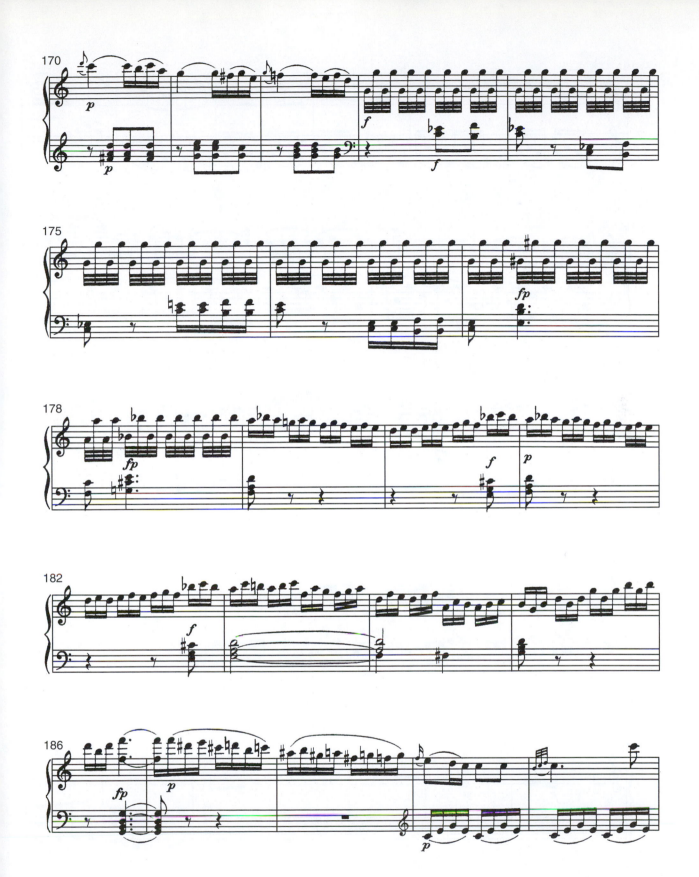

365. Sonata, op. 2, no. 3

Beethoven

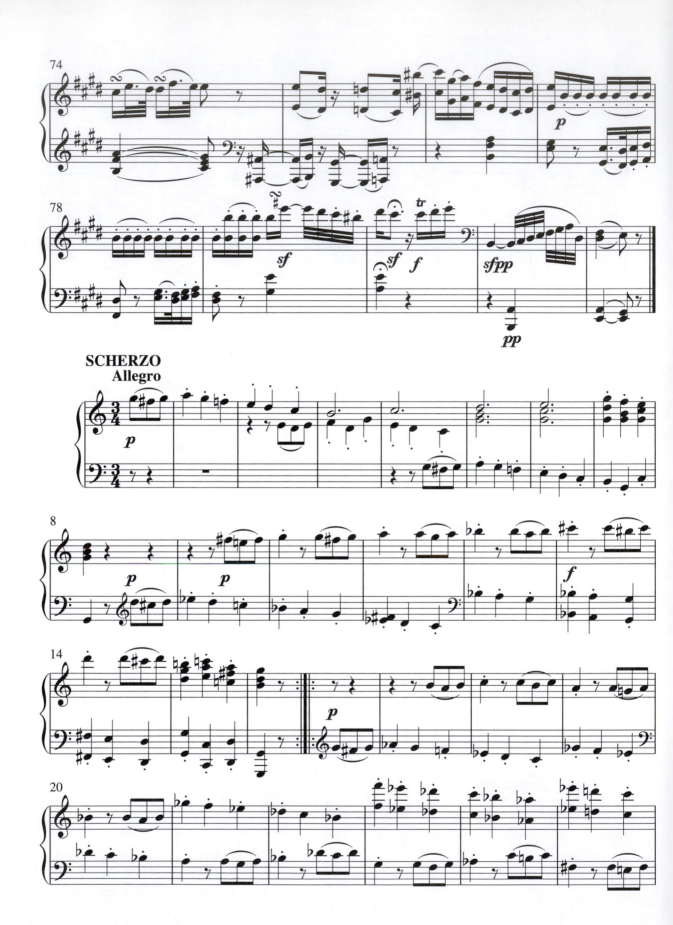

PART II. CHROMATIC MATERIALS

29. Examples of Counterpoint

Questions for Analysis

In this unit, in addition to the musical aspects you have been investigating, the following are also to be noted:

1. *Voice function and importance:* Are the voices equal and self-contained as lines? Do they have both independence and interdependence? Is there any feeling that one voice is ever supportive or accompanimental?
2. *Line:* Is each voice clearly shaped and motivically coherent? What are the melodic idioms at cadential points? Is melodic material shared between the voices?
3. *Harmony:* Is the harmony clear and functional? Are nonharmonic tones used consistently within the style? Is the harmonic rhythm steady? Are there any linear harmonies?
4. *Rhythm:* Is the meter clearly established and maintained? Are there rhythmic motives? Is there any sense of rhythmic growth through the phrase?
5. *Counterpoint:* What harmonic (vertical) intervals do you find on all beats and on the strongest beats? Are all dissonances and tendency tones resolved? What durational (rhythmic) ratios do you find between or among the voices? What directional relationships?
6. *Imitation:* Where there is imitation, what are the pitch interval and rhythmic interval between the entering voices? How long does the imitation continue?
7. *Sequence:* Are there sequences? How are they transposed? Are all voices involved? How many times are they repeated?
8. *Special techniques:* Are there any, such as stretto, melodic inversion, diminution, retrogression, or pedal point?

---

366. Cantata No. 4: Sinfonia

Bach

367. Chorale Prelude on "In Dulci Jubilo"*

Bach

*The chorale on which this prelude is based may be found in Unit 19, no. 232.

368. Chorale Prelude on "Christ lag in Todesbanden"*

Bach

*The chorale on which this prelude is based may be found in Unit 19, no. 233.

369. Chorale Prelude on "O wie selig seid ihr doch, ihr Frommen"

370. "Thy Hand Belinda", from *Dido and Aenas*

Purcell

371. Invention No. 4, BWV 775

Bach

372. Invention No. 13, BWV 775

Bach

373. Sinfonia 3, BWV 789

Bach

374. The Well-Tempered Clavier, Vol. I, Fugue 2

Bach

375. The Well-Tempered Clavier, Vol. II, Fugue 9

Bach

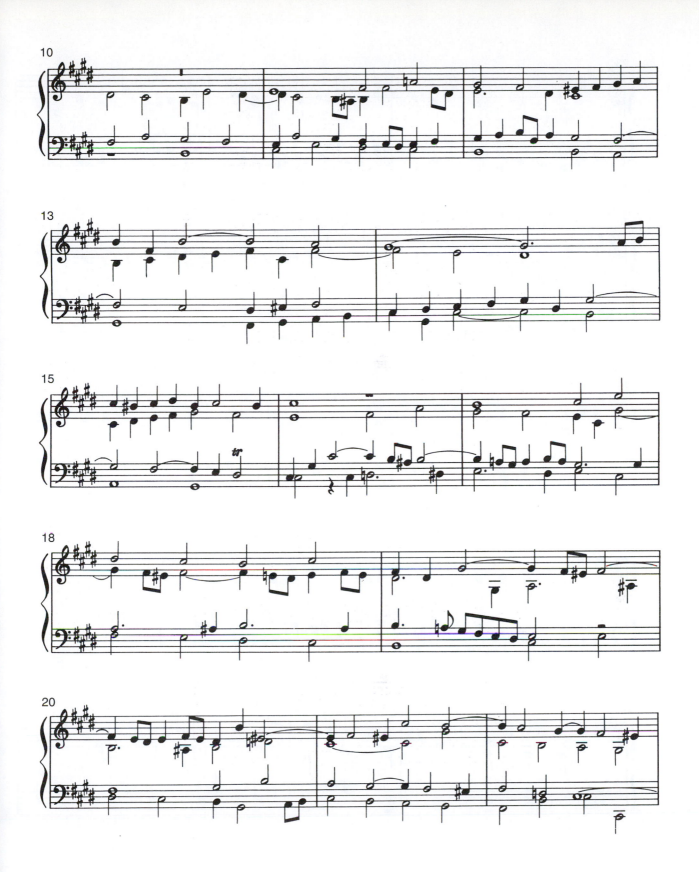

376. Fugue No. 2, op. 35

Tranquillo e sempre legato

Mendelsshon

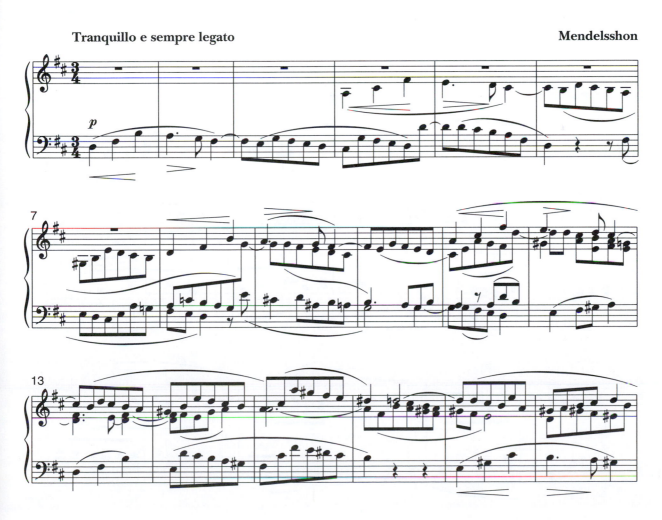

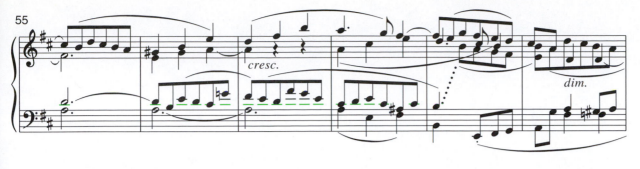

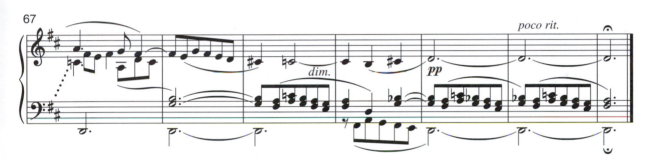

Additional Examples for the Study of Contrapuntal Techniques

162. Handel, *Leçon No.2, Minuet*

169. Purcell, *Rigadoon*

170. Witt, *Passacaglia*

199. Bach, *Christmas Oratorio, no. 4: Introduction*

200. Handel, *Sonata VII for Flute and Continuo, II*

231. Bach, *French Suite in C Minor*

232. Bach, *Wachet auf, ruft uns die Stimme*

233. Bach, *In dulci jubilo*

234. Bach, *Christ lag in Todesbanden*

235. Handel, *Menuet*

239. Handel, *Prelude*

261. Bach, *Invention No. 13*

269. Bach, *The Well Tempered Clavier, Vol. II, Fugue 17*

424. Hindemith, *Ludus Tonalis, Fuga secunda in G*

425. Bartók, *Concerto for Orchestra, I*

465. Hindemith, *Ludus Tonalis, Fuga undecima in B (Canon)*

III. Contemporary Materials

Suggestions for Discussion

Much of the music in this section can be heard and understood as an extension of common practice music, not necessarily requiring radically new methods of analysis. The underlying principles that unify older musics are still operative in this music, to a greater or lesser extent: traditional formal structures, cadences, regular phrase structures, and even at times periodic structure, motivic and gestural content, well-shaped melodies, rhythmic patterning and metric regularity, highly logical and consistent pitch organization, clear tonal centers, and so on. In many examples, the only nontraditional aspect is that of pitch relationships; in every other way much of this music is not very different in aesthetic or technique from that of the preceding several centuries.

At the same time, some new analytical approaches may be useful in understanding this music. With this in mind, each unit is prefaced by a few questions meant to guide your discussions and to suggest appropriate avenues of inquiry. These questions are by no means exhaustive, and many others will occur to you.

Additional Aspects to Consider

- Is there a tonal center, or centers, and how are they achieved (by line and harmony)? Do they change, and if so by what means?
- What formal structures are used—statement, departure, return; cadence and phrase structure; repetition, varied repetition, contrast, development?
- How are the pitches chosen? Is there a traditional or other scale or mode in use, and if so which? Is the scalar/harmonic material an extension of traditional tonal materials? Is the pitch organization purely intervallic? Is there a serial organization?
- What are the means of coherence—motivic, rhythmic, textural, registral, color, dynamic?
- How is the harmony structured? How are chords constructed (of what intervals)? How is their succession determined (any patterns)?
- How do counterpoint and voice leading play a role?
- Rhythm: Is the meter clear, and if so how is it made so? Are there any special effects (polyrhythm, polymeter, ametrical effects, isorhythmic patterns)?
- Be sure, as always, to discuss aspects of style, interrelation of the musical elements, and performance issues.

We would like again to direct your attention to the *Suggestions for Using This Book* on page xxii and to reiterate the importance of *hearing* the music in class and of discussing *all* the musical elements and their interactions.

1. Form and Theme: A B A. with each section roughly balanced: The two A sections. 8 measures each, are identical until the last measure. The four two-measures phrases form a kind of variation-chain, in which each phrase builds on and varies the thematic material of the preceding, making much out of very little material through varied repetition (in a typically Russian manner of composing).

The middle section (7 measures, mm. 9-15) contrasts strongly in tempo, mood, dynamic and (to some extent) musical materials. Yet at the same time its main thematic and motivic materials (mm. 9-10) are clearly related to the pitch materials and rhythm of the A section. This balancing of contrasting and unifying elements in the B section is typical of good compositions.

Measures 12-15 form a cadenza-like transition back to A, emphasizing the modal "dominant" of F♯ aeolian, C♯ (left hand) and E (the modal subtonic, right hand). Like many brief B sections, the emphasis is on dominant prolongation.

Proper labeling of the overall form is not easy. The first A section is open-ended (ending on dominant harmony): the B section, while contrasting, is still not capable of standing alone as an independent work; even the closing A is open-ended harmonically. Proportionally, the piece is not rounded binary, nor is it ternary, because of the unstable and brief quality of the B section. This may be best described as a continuous ternary structure, with elements of variation process.

The climactic music is in mm. 14-15, supported by register, texture rhythmic activity and dynamic. The placement (about 3/4 of the way through) and harmony (dominant prolongation) of the climax are typical of many works.

2. Tonal center and scale. The tonal center is clearly F♯, and the mode is aeolian. The two E♯'s (mm. 7-8 and 22-23) create some ambiguity as to whether this is also in F♯ minor. This mixture of modality and tonality is typical of many early twentieth-century works. Except for the two leading tones, the work is entirely diatonic. The tonic pitch is made clear in the main theme, which circles around it and back, and in the emphasis on F♯ and C♯ in the harmony and bass line. Measures 1 and 2, then 3 and 4 begin and end on tonic harmony, and m. 8 on dominant (a medial or progressive cadence, related to a tonal half-cadence).

3. Harmony. The work overall is stabilized by harmony that moves between tonic and dominant pitches in the lowest voice: as B section prolongs the dominant, neighboring the C♯ in the left hand, and the F♯ center returns with the return of A. The end is unresolved, with the melodic line ending on tonic but the supporting harmony on subdominant, which echoes the subdominant quality of the harmony in mm. 1, 3, 5-6., and the neighboring harmonies of the B section. Harmonies emphasizing E natural, the subtonic scale degree (mm. 2, 4 and throughout the B section) are typical of modal harmony; the use of the leading tone is thus especially striking. The vocabulary is made up of diatonic triads (sometimes in non-traditional positions, such as the 6/4 in mm. 2 and 4) and seventh-chords (the leading-tone seventh chord in mm. 7-8 at the medial cadence), the minor seventh chords in the B section, built on scale degrees 4 and 5, and functioning in a way analogous to subdominant and dominant harmonies.

Note the planing of the seventh chords in measures 9 and 11.

4. Structure. The upper voice prolongs A, with an upper neighbor B, descends to G♯ at the end of the first A, prolongs A and E in the B section, and repeats its motion in the return of A. The overall line is thus scale degrees $\hat{3}$ – $\hat{4}$ – $\hat{3}$ – $\hat{2}$; $\hat{3}$ – $\hat{4}$ – $\hat{3}$ – $\hat{2}$ – $\hat{1}$.

The lower voice emphasizes the tonic and dominant degrees, and the upper and lower neighbors to the dominant. It ends inconclusively on the subdominant (is the shepherd retreating into the distance, perhaps to return later?).

30. Extended and Altered Tertian Harmony

Questions for Analysis

1. Does functional (roman numeral) analysis apply to any of these excerpts? Are keys and chord structures clear and in traditional relationships? Are some other pitch descriptive systems more useful here, such as jazz/pop chord symbols?
2. In what other ways are these excerpts similar to common practice music? Consider form, phrase structure, motive, theme, counterpoint, and so on.
3. In what ways do they represent departures from older techniques?

---

377. Symphony No. 2, op. 30
I, reh. F

Hanson

---

378. Sonatina, op. 13

Kabalevsky

379. Mysterious Mountain
I, m. 12

Hovhaness

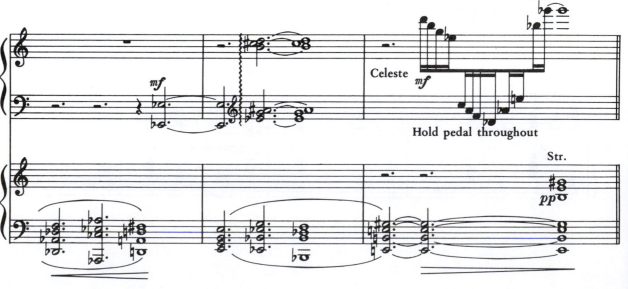

380. Prelude, op. 34, no. 24

Shostakovich

381. Pelléas et Mélisande, Act I, scene 1
m. 178

Debussy

30. EXTENDED AND ALTERED TERTIAN HARMONY   407

382. Poem, op. 32, no. 2

Scriabin

383. Valses Nobles et Sentimentales
m. 53

Ravel

---

384. Slaughter on Tenth Avenue

Junior dances with Vera's dead body.

Andante doloroso

Rodgers

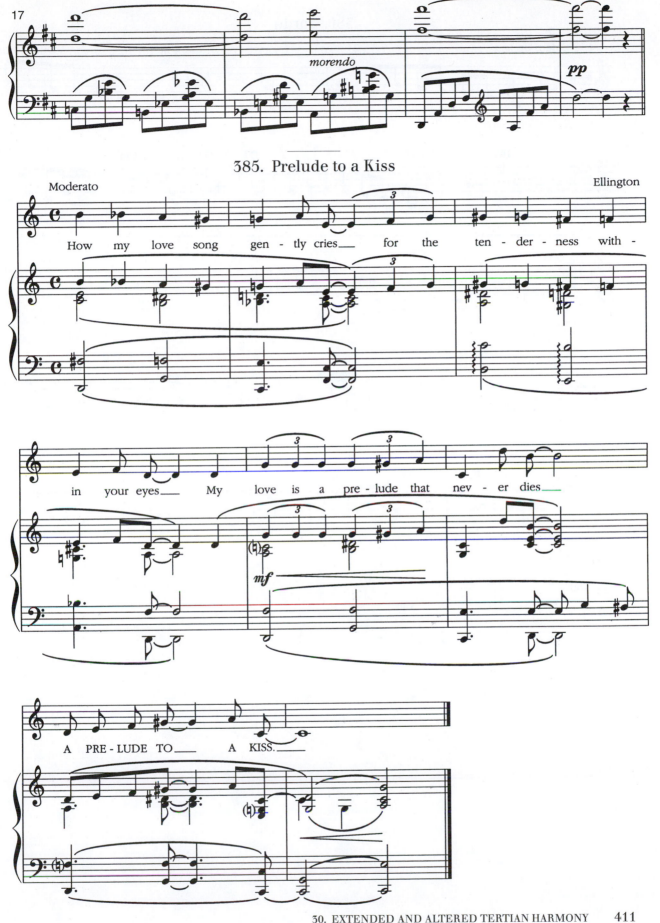

385. Prelude to a Kiss

Moderato

Ellington

How my love song gen - tly cries___ for the ten - der - ness with -

in your eyes___ My love is a pre - lude that nev - er dies___

A PRE - LUDE TO___ A KISS.

386. Jordu

387. Four Songs, op. 2, no. 3

Erst ziemlich bewegt, dann langsam

Berg

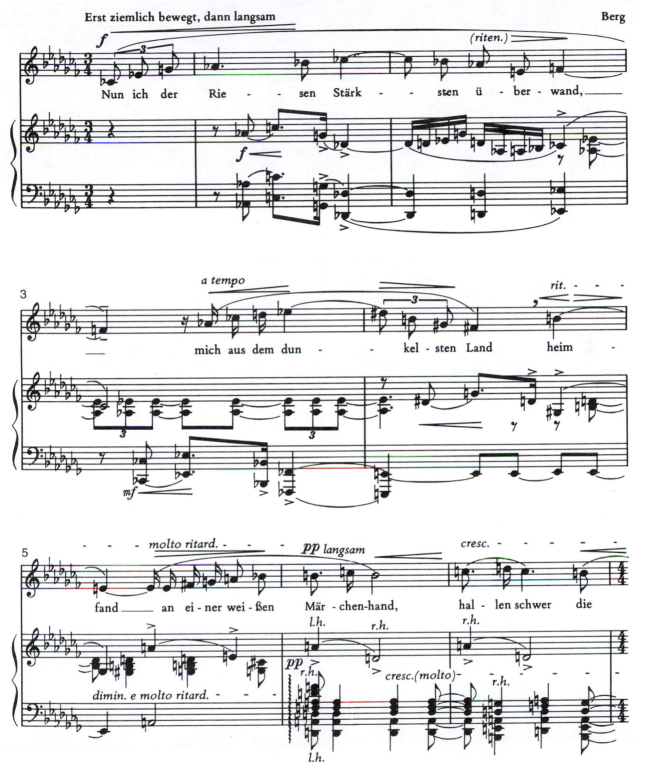

Now that I have defeated the strongest of giants, have found my way home
from the darkest land on a white fairy-tale hand, the bells sound heavily and
I stagger through the alleys, caught in sleep.

388. Laura

Raksin

31. Diatonic (Church) Modes

Model Analysis

Bartók, *Dance from for Children, Book II*

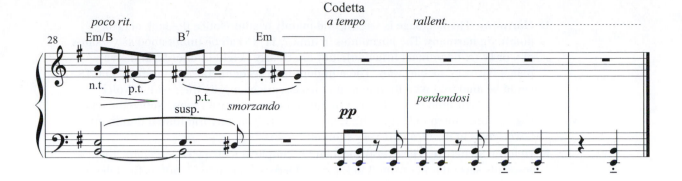

Observations:

A. **Form**: Introduction (mm. 1-4), A (mm. 5-12), A^1 (mm. 13-20). A^2 (mm. 22-30), Codetta (mm. 31-34)

 – The Introduction establishes tonal center, mode (Aeolian), meter, tempo, harmonic language, ostinato pattern, character (dance-like) and prolongs tonic harmony. The Codetta balances the Introduction and frames the composition, providing confirmation of ostinato pattern and tonal center, as well as very clear end-shaping through a built-in ritardando using note values, tempo marking and dynamics.

 – The A sections are all divided into regular 4 measure phrases which could be shown as a and a^1; the cadence ending the a phrase is medial (or progressive; it ends on scale 5, requires continuation and is analogous to a half cadence in tonal music); the cadence ending the a^1 phrase is more final, ending on the tonal center. These phrases throughout could be heard as constituting parallel periods. Because the A section is heard, with harmonic variants, three times, there is a high degree of thematic unification.

 – mm. 21 and 22 are the only break from the 4-bar phrase length. Measure 21 is an "extra" measure at the end of a phrase; its harmony (a "misspelled" German augmented-sixth chord) implics harmonic movement to dominant, so that the phrase modulation to G major in the next bar is especially surprising. This chord in effect resolves in m. 28. Measure 22 is a highly compressed "introduction" to the G major harmonization of the melody.

B. **Motive and Theme**. There is a high degree of motivic and thematic consistency. The rhythmic ostinato provides a regular underpinning. One could hear three main motives, mm. 5, 6, and 7(which is treated sequentially), and these provide all the melodic material. Contrast and variety are provided mainly by harmonic changes under the melody, by dynamics, articulations and tempo variants.

C. **Tonal center and scale**. This is clearly in some version of E minor, but notice the absence of any instance of the pitch-class D until m. 16; until m. 26, the effect is of the E natural minor scale or Aeolian mode. The D♯ implies a more traditional E minor scale, but is short and weak, so an ambiguity remains.

 The **modulation** to the temporary tonal center of G major is accomplished by assertion (the pedal ostinato in mm. 22-26), the pivot note B in m. 23, and the fact that the melody can easily be heard in G major as well as E minor. The modulation back to E minor is accomplished by pivot note in m. 27, and the fact that m. 28 resolves m. 21 harmonically. This music in G major sounds like a brief interpolation or "trope" of music in the relative key.

D. Harmony. The language is tertian, and mainly triadic. Notice the lack of clear dominant harmony. The harmonies in mm. 7, 11, 15 can be understood as versions of ii or IV (subdominant function); they are clearly neighbor chords, and give a plagal flavor to the harmony. The non-dominant seventh chords in mm. 16 and 18 could be analyzed with Roman numerals, but are primarily the result of voice-leading linear motion, made clear in the melodic structure graph. Notice the tenor-register line, surrounding B with C and Bb (=A#). The only traditional dominant harmony is in m. 29, and is very short and weak.

E. Melodic Structure. The overall structure is simple and clear. The melodic line descends several times from B to E (scale-degrees 5 down to 1), but its final descent occurs in measures 27-30. Thus the local (period-length) and overall linear structure are identical. The bass-line is very traditional, prolonging tonic (mm. 1-15), then descending diatonically (scale degrees 1, 7, 6), finally arriving at the dominant note in m. 28 (following the "detour" to G major), and then returns to tonic.

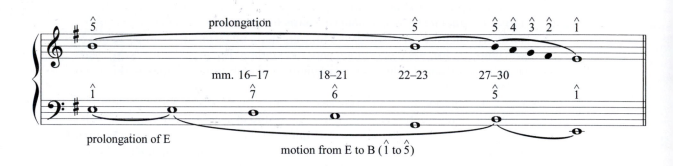

Questions for Analysis

1. By what means are the tonal center and mode made clear?
2. Are there instances of mixing, layering, or shifting of modes within any excerpt?
3. What sorts of harmonic structures are present? Are they always clearly tertian?

---

389. Little Pieces for Children, no. III

Bartók

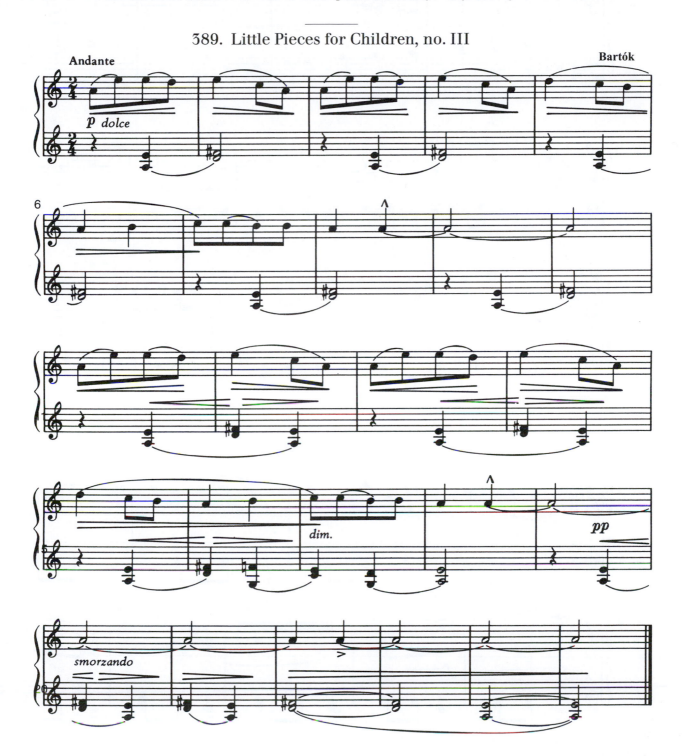

390. Ten Preludes, no. 1

Andantino espressivo ♩ = 84

Chávez

391. Valse

Assez vif

Poulenc

392. Trois Chansons, no. 1

Très modéré, soutenu et expressif

Debussy

Dieu! qu'il la fait bon re - gar - der La gra - ci - eu - se bonne et

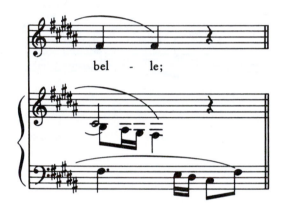

bel - le;

God! He has made her attractive, gracious, good, and beautiful.

393. Toccatina

Allegretto

Kabalevsky

394. Ceremony of Carols, no. 8

Britten

395. Suite bergamasque: Passepied

Allegretto ma non troppo

Debussy

396. Susannah, Act II, scene 3

Andante piangendo (♪ = 96)

Susannah

Floyd

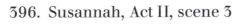

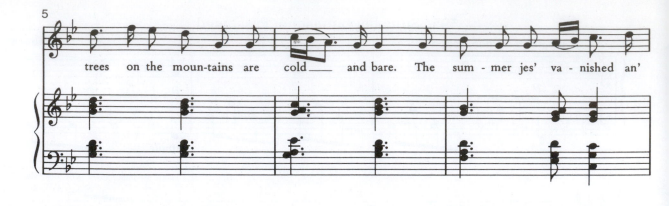

trees ___ on the moun-tains are cold ___ and bare. The sum - mer jes' va - nished an'

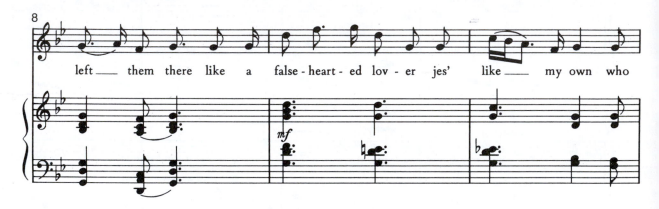

left ___ them there like a false - heart - ed lov - er jes' like ___ my own who

made me love _ him, then left _ me a - lone.

___

397. Five Fingers: Lento

Stravinsky

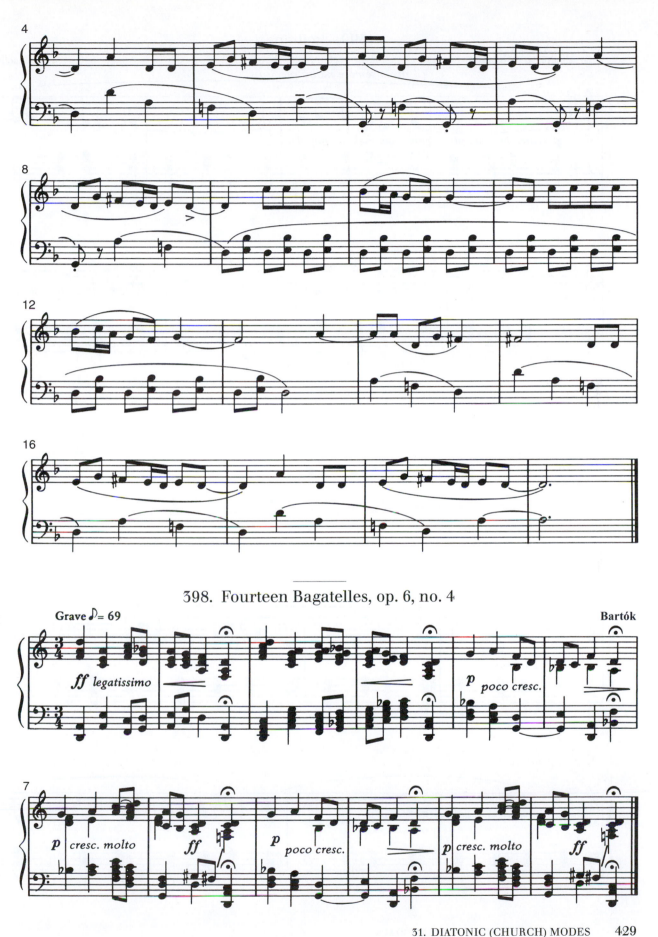

398. Fourteen Bagatelles, op. 6, no. 4

Grave ♪= 69

ff legatissimo

p poco cresc.

Bartók

p cresc. molto

ff

p poco cresc.

p cresc. molto

ff

399. Siciliana

Allegretto dolcemente mosso
(il ritmo sempre molto preciso)

Casella

400. Work Song

Adderley

32. Pandiatonicism and Additive Harmony

Questions for Analysis

1. Is Roman numeral analysis applicable to any of these excerpts? What other systems of harmonic description might also be helpful? Are all these excerpts essentially tertian?
2. What scales and/or modes do you find? By what means are scale and mode made clear?
3. What elements distinguish this music from common practice music using the same materials?

401. Mother Goose Suite: The Magic Garden

402. Touches Blanches

Milhaud

403. The Irishman Dances

Cowell

404. The Young Pioneers
m. 32

Quite fast

Copland

405. Excursions, III
m. 49

Allegretto ♩ = 60

Barber

406. Petroushka: Danse Russe

Allegro giusto ♩= 116

Stravinsky

407. Gloria: Laudamus te

Poulenc

We praise thee.

33. Exotic (Artificial, Synthetic) Scales

Questions for Analysis

1. How are tonal center and scale made clear?
2. What are the interval characteristics of each scale? What intervals are missing from any given scale? What effect does this have on the music? What analytic systems (Hanson, Persichetti, interval vector) might be useful in understanding this music?
3. Is there any shifting, mixing, or changing of scales within any excerpt?

408. Touches Noires

409. Mikrokosmos, no. 78: Five Tone Scale

410. Valsette

411. London Symphony
I, Reh. M

Vaughan Williams

412. Préludes, II: Voiles

Debussy

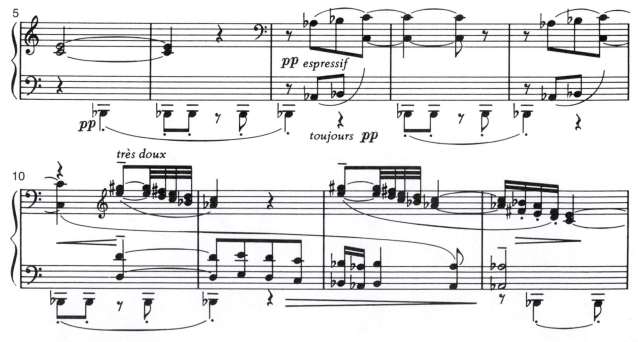

413. Mikrokosmos, no. 136: Whole Tone Scale

Andante, ♩ = 108

Bartók

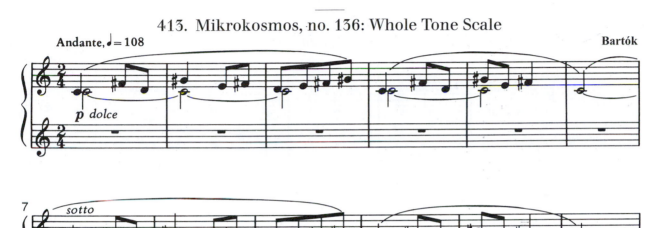

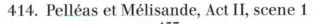

414. Pelléas et Mélisande, Act II, scene 1
m. 137

Lento

Debussy

415. Fourteen Bagatelles, op. 6, no. 10
m. 10

416. Bucolic, no. 3
m. 20

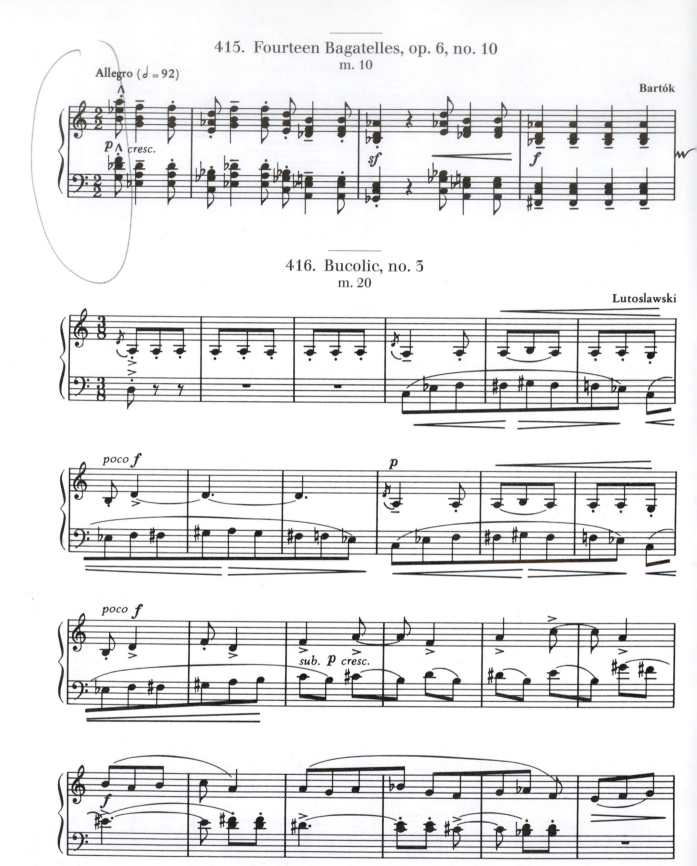

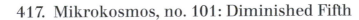

417. Mikrokosmos, no. 101: Diminished Fifth

Bartók

418. Sketches, op. 9, no. 6

419. Fourteen Bagatelles, op. 6, no. 6

34. Quartal and Secundal Harmony

Questions for Analysis

1. What sorts of interval structures are used to organize each excerpt? How consistent are they within each? Does each have a clear tonal center and if so, how is it emphasized?
2. What new analytic systems would be applicable to this music? Consider pitch and interval class analysis, Hanson, Persichetti, and perhaps others.
3. What are the traditional and nontraditional elements in each excerpt? Make lists of both aspects.

420. Mathis der Maler: Grablegung

Hindemith

421. Majority
m. 20

Ives

The Mas - ses   are   think - ing,   Whence comes the thought   of   the   World!

422. Piano Piece, op. 39, no. 5

Krenek

423. Ludus Tonalis, Fuga secunda in G

Hindemith

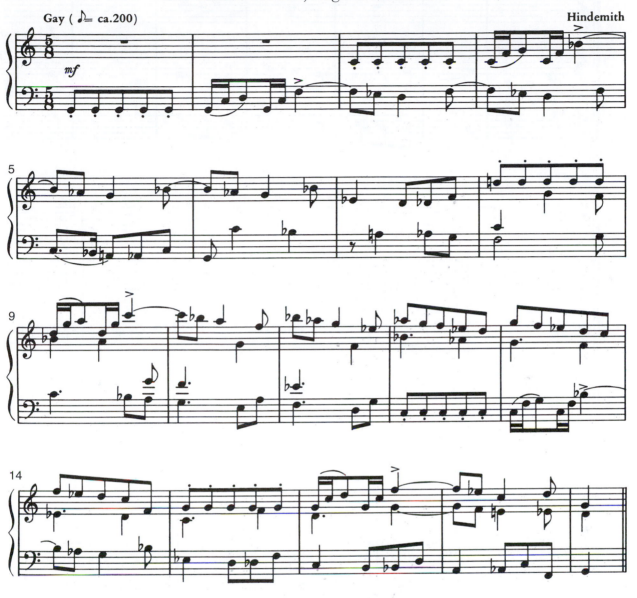

424. Concerto for Orchestra
I, m. 316

Bartók

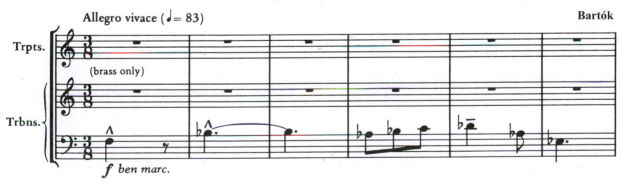

425. Wozzeck, Act II

Langsam (♪.=56-60) aber nicht schleppend

Berg

Marie *p*

Mä - del, was fangst Du jetzt an?_____ Hast ein klein Kind und kein

Mann!_____ Ei, was frag' ich dar - nach,_____

Sing'_____ ich die gan - ze Nacht.

"Maiden, what are you doing now? You have a small child and no husband.
Oh, what are you asking for?" I sing the whole night through.

426. Mikrokosmos, no. 107: Melody in the Mist

427. Wozzeck, Act II

A hunter from the palace once rode through a green wood.

428. Tiger

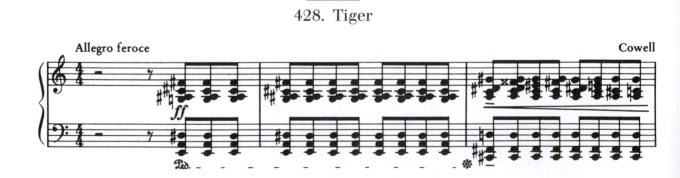

Cowell

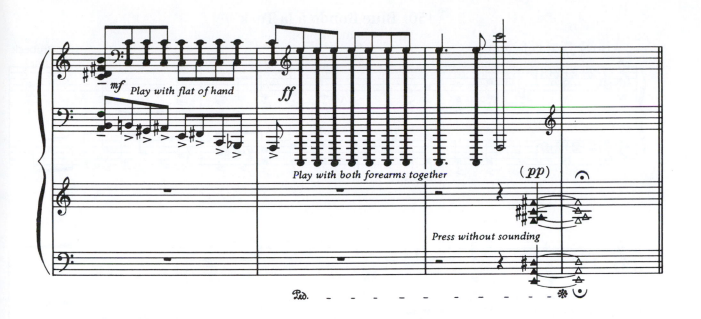

Play with flat of hand

Play with both forearms together

Press without sounding

(pp)

---

429. Majority

Ives

Slowly

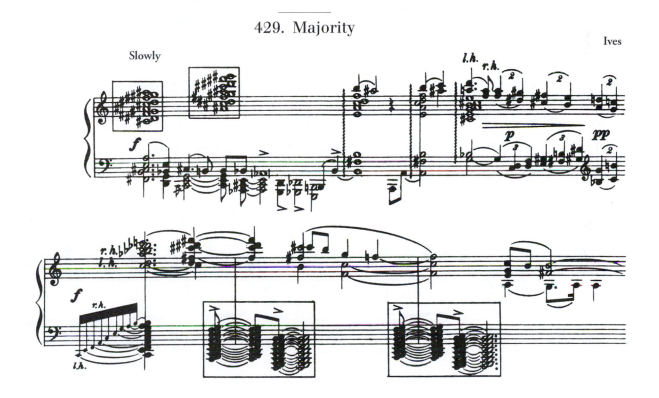

430. Blue Rondo à la Turk
m. 57

Brubeck

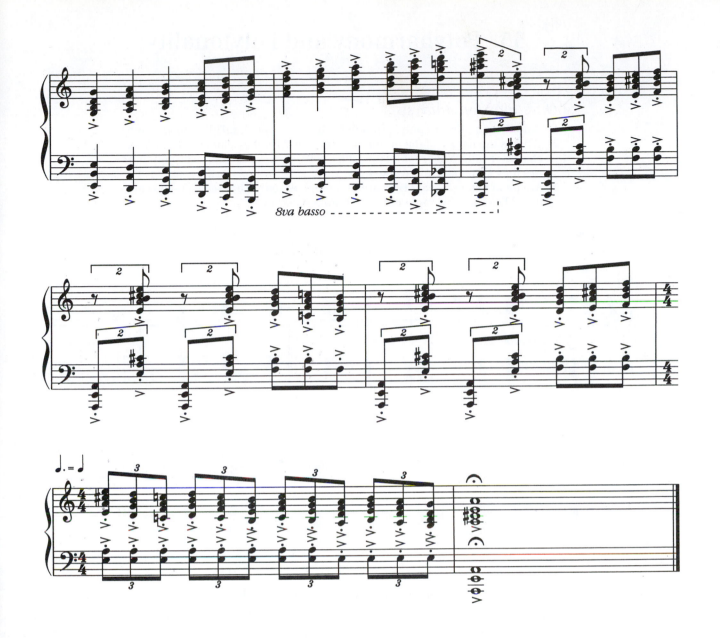

35. Polyharmony and Polytonality

Questions for Analysis

1. Which examples are polyharmonic? Which are polytonal? Which are both?
2. What is the nature of the harmonic structures? Do they combine traditional chords or not? What root relationships between keys or chords do you find? Are they systematically worked out?
3. Are tonal centers clear? How are they emphasized? What scale systems are used? Does any example *not* use a traditional scale?

------

431. Symphony No. 5
I

------

432. A Three-Score Set, II

433. Allegro Giocoso
m. 31

Kraft

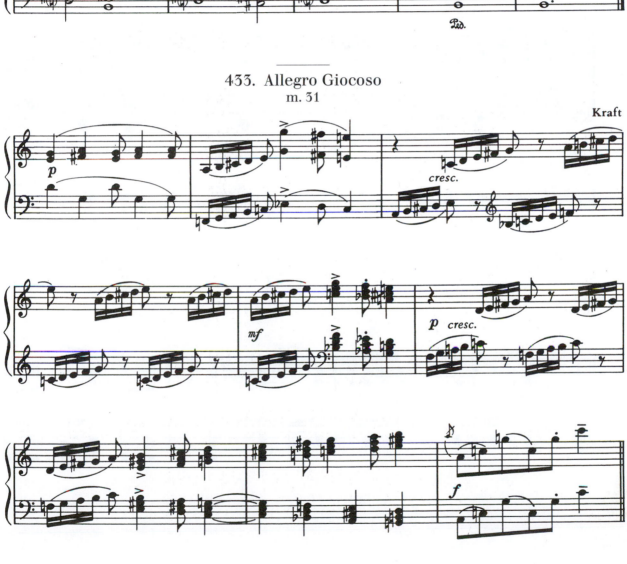

434. The Rake's Progress: Prelude

Stravinsky

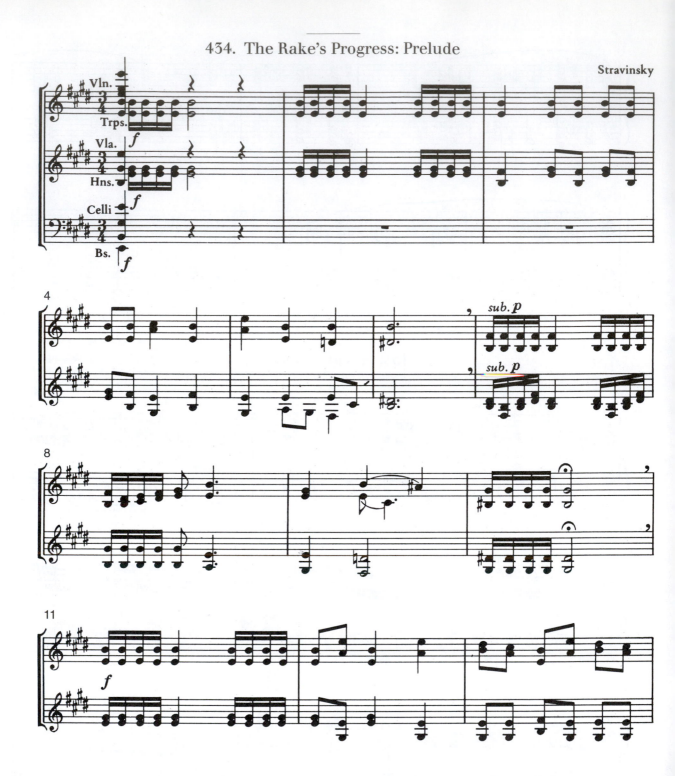

435. Petroushka, Scene 2
Reh. 95, m. 9

Stravinsky

436. Saudades do Brazil, no. 7: Corcovado
m. 19

Milhaud

437. Forty-Four Violin Duets, no. 33

Bartók

438. Strange Meadowlark
m. 37

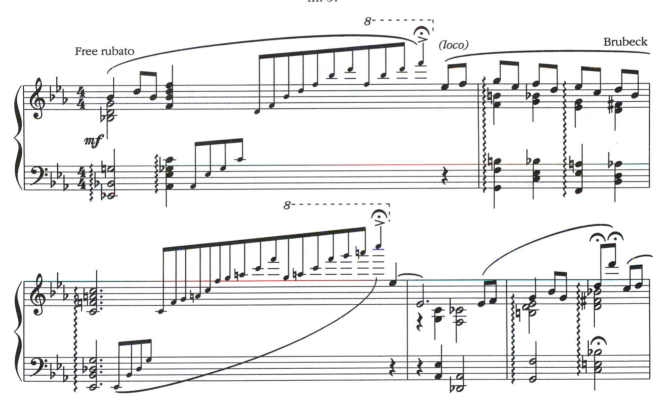

36. Free Atonality

Questions for Analysis

1. This sort of music is often referred to as "atonal," but are there perceptible tonal centers in any of these excerpts? If so, how are these established?
2. Which intervallic "cells" or sets are used to unify each example? To what extent do these seem consistent? Which intervals in each seem important? Which less so? Apply set-theoretic (pitch- and interval-class and interval vector) analysis.
3. What are the other means of unification? Consider theme, gesture, motive, phrase structure, register, rhythm, and so on.

439. Drei Klavierstücke, op. 11, no. 1

440. Klavierstücke, op. 19, no. 2

441. Pierrot Lunaire, op. 21, no. 1: Mondestrunken

Schönberg

The wine one drinks with one's eyes
Pours down nightly in waves from the moon.
And a spring-tide flood washes over
The silent horizon.

442. Five Movements for String Quartet, op. 5, no. 4

Webern

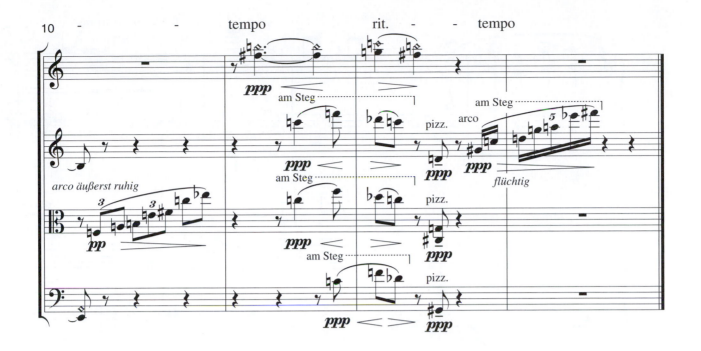

443. Mikrokosmos, no. 144: Minor Seconds, Major Sevenths

Bartók

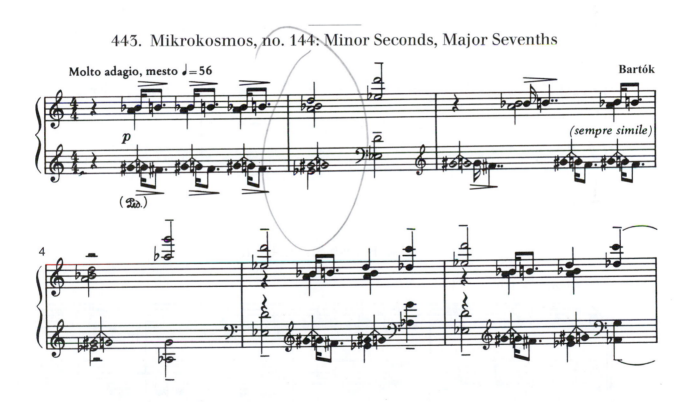

444. Fourth String Quartet

I

Allegro, ♩= 110

Bartók

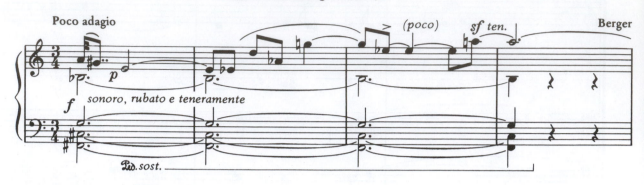

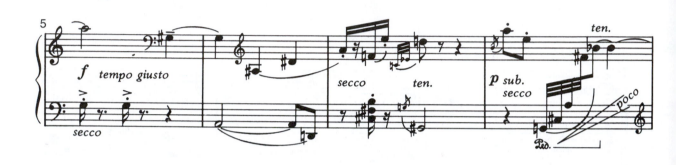

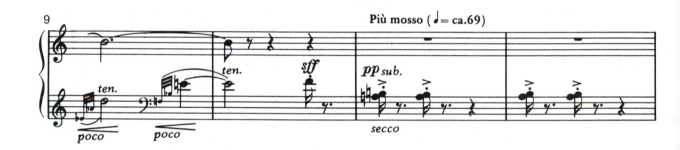

445. Two Episodes, I

Berger

37. Twelve-Tone Serialism

Model Analysis

Schönberg, *Fourth String Quarter, op. 37, I*

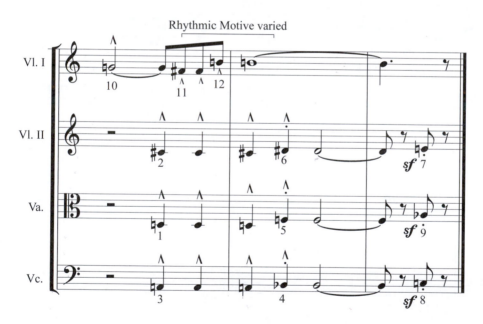

Row: P₀

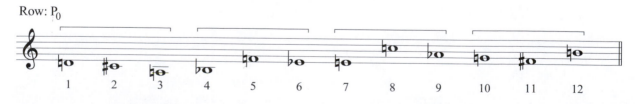

Observations:

A. The texture is melody with a rhythmically patterned chordal accompaniment.

B. This example has a single phrase. The sense of cadence is established by the long B♮ in the 1st violin along with the repeated quarter notes and tied half note in the lower voices, punctuated by the final eighth note *sf* chord.

C. The row is segmented into groups of three notes. These subsets are used to form the accompanying chords. Chords consistently use the same three pitch-classes, but the pitches are reordered from high to low for variety. The specific chords, and their order within the measure, always provides the complement to the three pitch-classes occuring in the melody, thus assuring that each measure will contain the complete row with no duplication of pitches.

D. There is a prominent rhythmic motive in the solo part, but the melodic shape of the motive is dependent upon the row and the composer's decisions as to register for a given pitch class.

Questions for Analysis

1. For each excerpt, label each row-form at its beginning, using whatever system your instructor suggests; number each note in the row. Write down each row (in terms of pitch-class integers or letter names) or construct a magic square (matrix), if your instructor so requests. What are the interval characteristics of each row? What melodic and harmonic intervals are emphasized in the music? Is the row always consistently and fully used? Are the pitches always in order? Does a statement of the row coincide with some sort of structural articulation, such as a phrase or motivic statement?

2. Where different row-forms are used in the same piece, successively or simultaneously, why are these particular forms (and not others) used? Consider such issues as pitch-class invariants, segmentation of rows, and combinatoriality.

3. Aside from the serial aspects, what traditional organizing elements are found in each excerpt? Consider form, phrase, theme, motive, rhythm, gesture, meter, and so on.

---

446. Dancing Toys, op. 83, no. 1

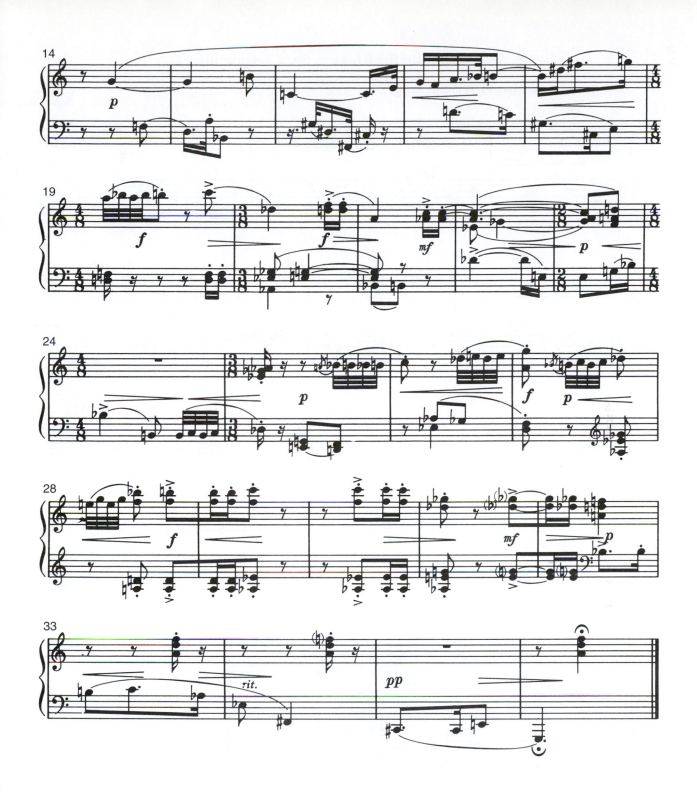

447. Suite für Klavier, op. 25: Gavotte

Etwas langsam ($\downarrow$ = ca.72) nicht hastig

Schönberg

448. Cinque Frammenti di Saffo

Dallapiccola

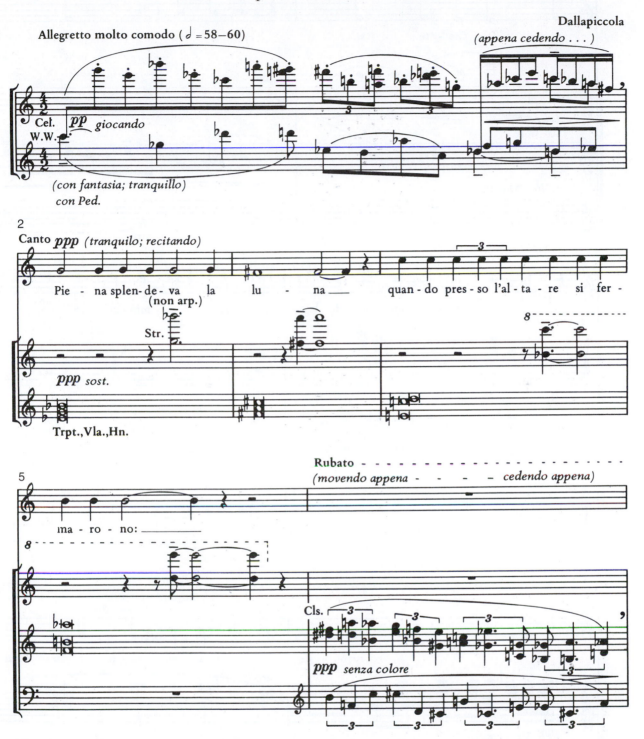

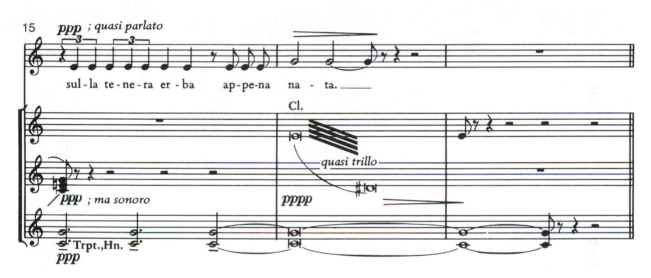

Full shone the moon, when by the altar they stopped. And the Cretian woman, with music, upon light feet, began carefree to go about the altar, upon the tender young grass.

449. Drei Lieder, op. 25, no. 1

How happy I am! Once again everything becomes green and glowing to me!
Still the flowers bloom over all my world! Once again I have been placed
entirely in becoming and am on the earth.

38. Music Since 1945*

Questions for Analysis

1. Listen carefully and repeatedly to the assigned examples. What elements of pitch organization are present? What other aspects of unification are used?
2. In what ways are the nonpitch aspects of any given example important? Consider texture, color, register, rhythmic activity (attack and sustain density), dynamics, and so on.
3. What nontraditional ways of performing and of listening are called for in these excerpts?

---

450. Klavierstücke, no. 2

Stockhausen

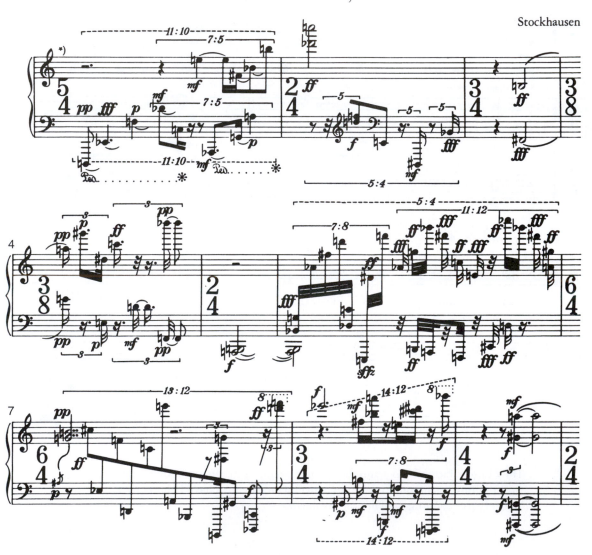

*For explanation of new notational procedures, see complete scores of the pieces included in this unit and *Music Notation in the Twentieth Century* by Kurt Stone (New York: W. W. Norton, 1980).

---

451. String Quartet (1965)
m. 33

Lutoslawski

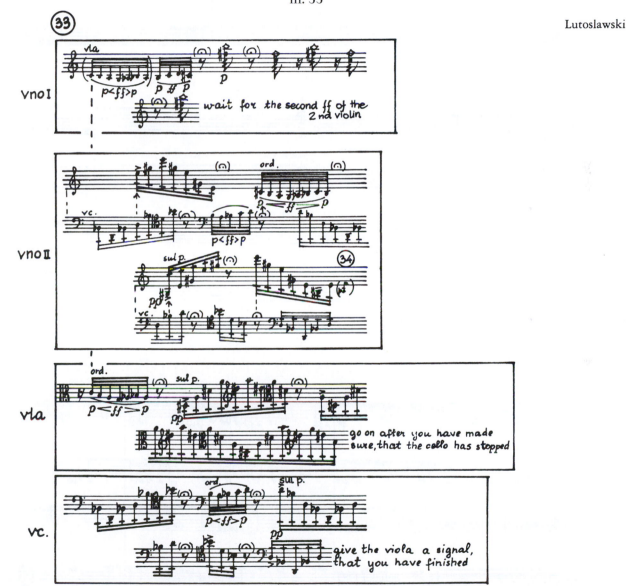

452. String Quartet, no. 2

Vivace

Penderecki

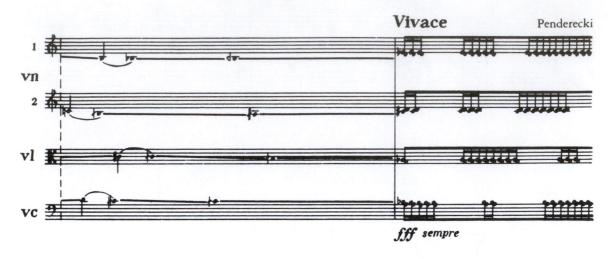

fff sempre

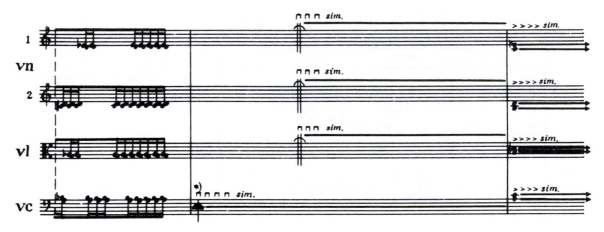

*) mit dem Bogen auf der rechten Schmalseite des Steges spielen
bow the right narrow side of the bridge

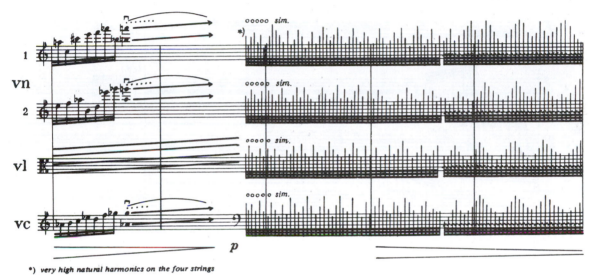

*) very high natural harmonics on the four strings

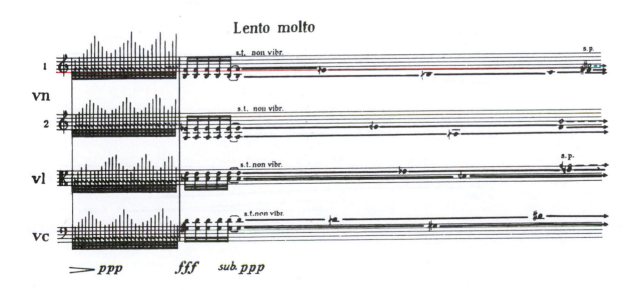

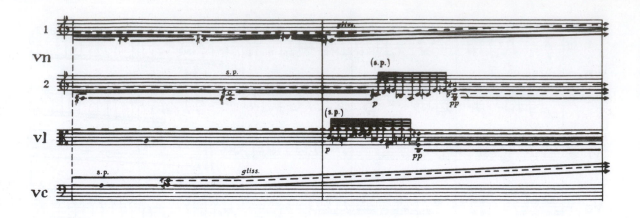

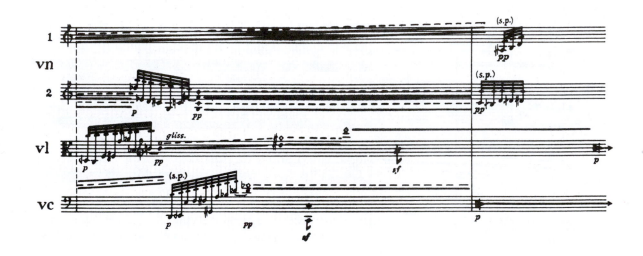

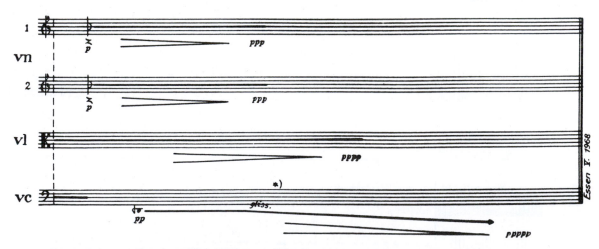

*) during the glissando turn slowly down the turning peg

II. Tu cuerpo, con la sombra violeta de mis manos, era un arcángel de frío
[Through my hands violet shadow, your body was an archangel, cold]

CRUMB

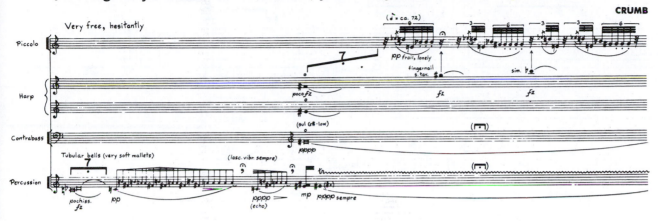

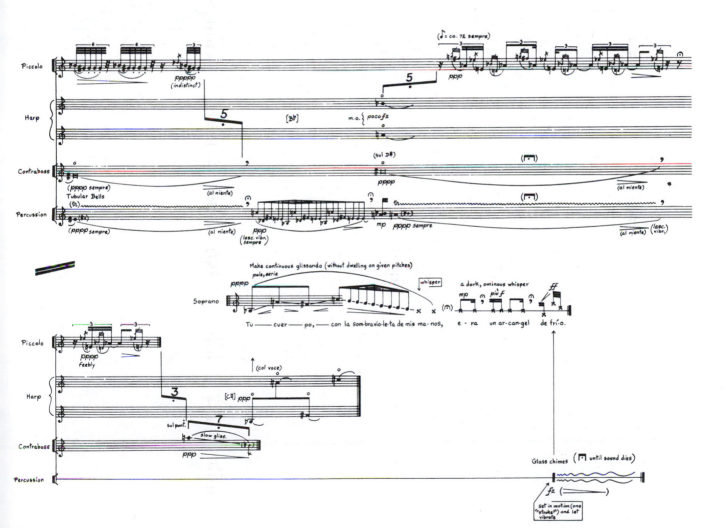

454. Valentine, for solo contrabass

DRUCKMAN

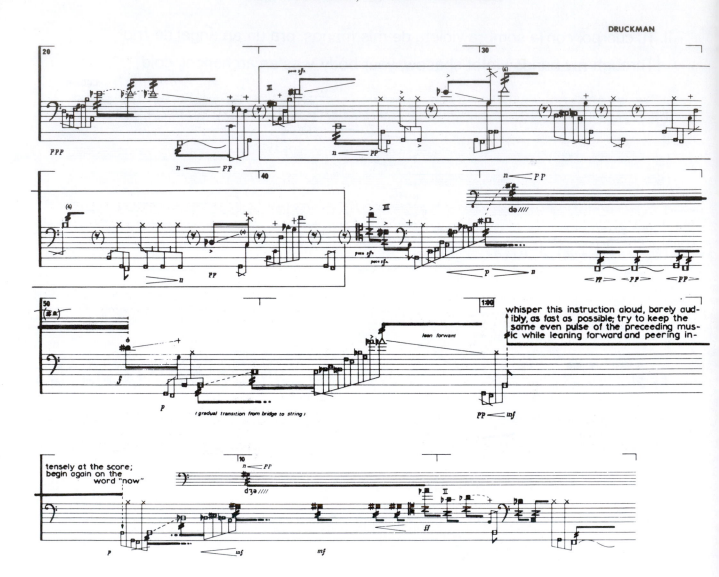

whisper this instruction aloud, barely aud-
ibly, as fast as possible; try to keep the
same even pulse of the preceeding music while leaning forward and peering in-

tensely at the score;
begin again on the
word "now"

(gradual transition from bridge to string)

455. Valentine

Rouse

Solo Flute

456. Six Short Studies, Sixteenth Notes

Horne

(fade almost to nothing)

39. Complete Pieces for Analysis IV

Suggestion for Analysis

In the preceding units of Part III, various materials and techniques of the twentieth century appeared in isolation. In the complete pieces in this unit, however, you will find combinations of these materials and techniques within a single work. As a first step, identify these materials and techniques. Then, proceed to analyze this music as you did with the complete pieces in earlier units.

---

457. Sonatine, Mouv^t II

458. Pour le Piano: Sarabande

459. Préludes, X: La Cathédrale engloutie

459

Debussy

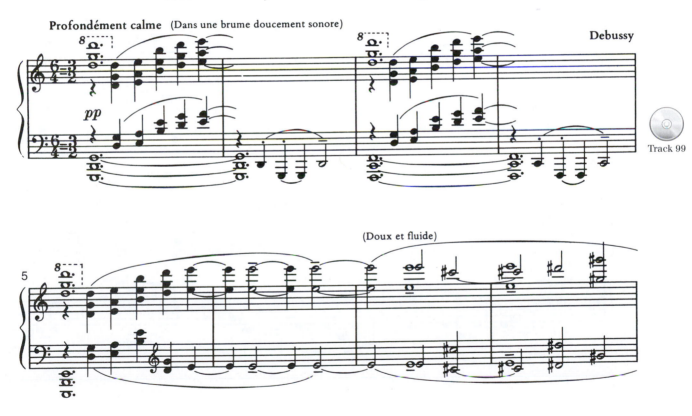

Track 99

Un peu moins lent (Dans une expression allant grandissant)

460. Saudades do Brazil, No. 6. Gavea

Milhaud

Ne garder la Pédale que sur la 1ʳᵉ moitié de la mesure

461. Classical Symphony, op. 25
III

Prokofiev

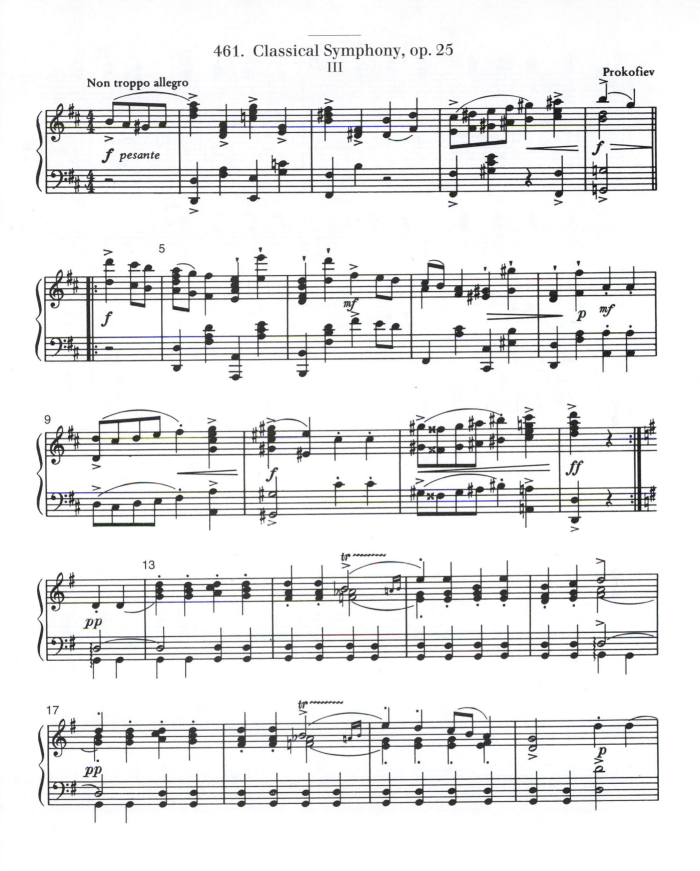

462. March from The Love of Three Oranges

Prokofiev

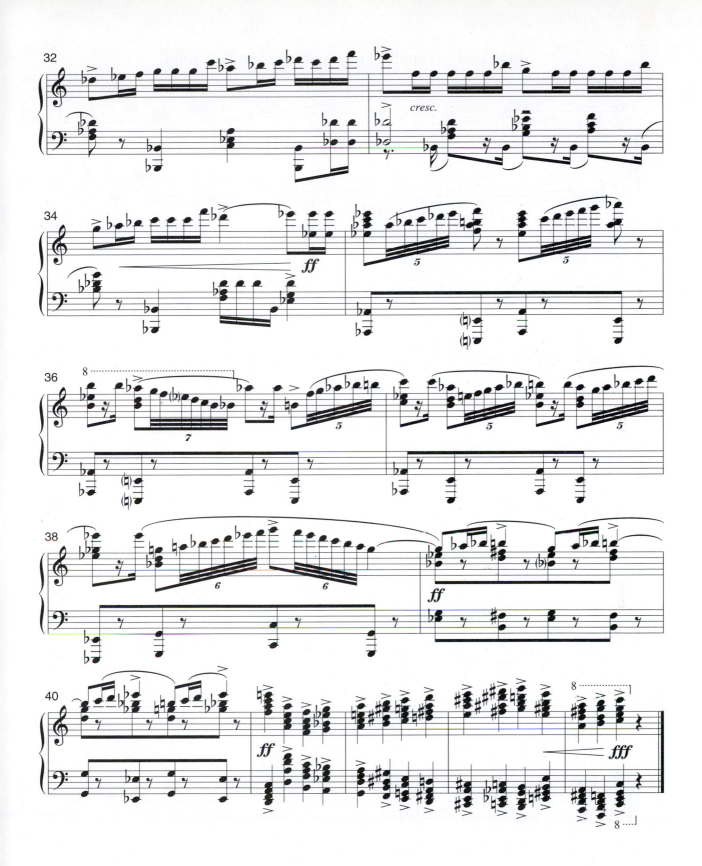

463. Ludus Tonalis, Fuga undecima in B (Canon)

Slow (♩ ca.54)

Hindemith

464. Evocations, no. 1

Ruggles

465. Suite für Klavier, op. 25: Menuett

Schönberg

466. Night and Day

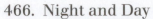

Moderato

Porter

Like the beat, beat, beat of the tom - tom, When the jun - gle shad - ows

fall, Like the tick, tick, tock of the state - ly clock, As it

stands a - gainst the wall, Like the drip, drip, drip of the

63

let me spend my life mak-ing love___ to you, day and night,_____ night and day._

67

1.

2.

Night and day___ _____

467. Porgy and Bess, "Summertime"

Gershwin

Allegretto semplice

mf espressivo

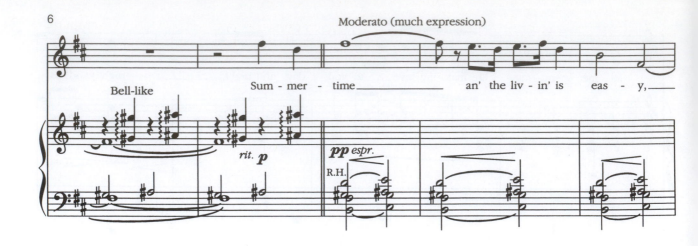

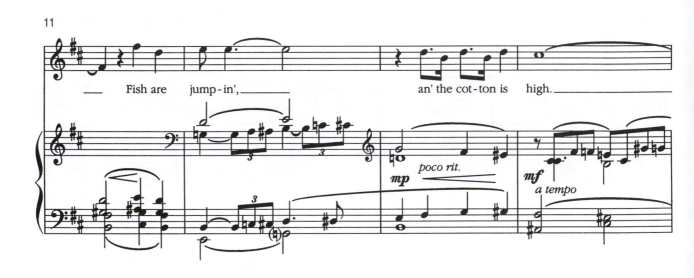

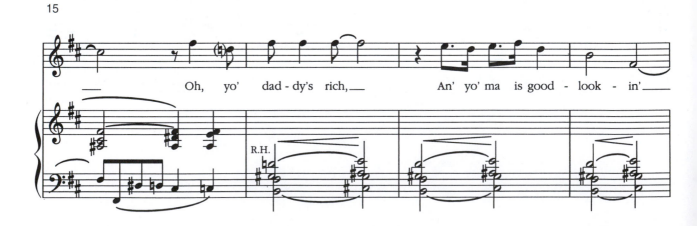

an' you'll take____ the sky._____ But till that

morn - in'_____ there's a noth - in' can harm you_____ With

Dad - dy an' Mam - my stand - in' by._____

468. Sonata for Two Pianos, II: Theme with Variations

Stravinsky

Variation 1

Variation 2

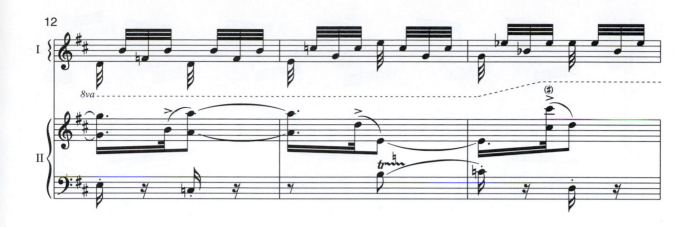

Variation 3

Variation 4
conclusion

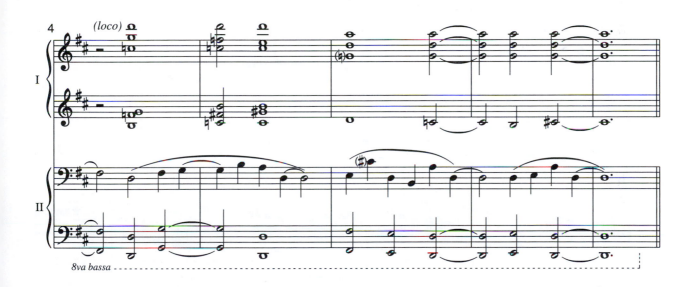

39. COMPLETE PIECES FOR ANALYSIS IV   541

469. Piano Sonata No.2

I

Hindemith

470. Piano Sonata, I

Macmillan

Appendix A

Checklist for Analysis and Sample Analysis*

All music should be analyzed as fully as possible within the limits of the student's knowledge at any stage of learning. Not only the individual elements but also their interactions should be studied. Following is a checklist of elements that should be included in an analysis.

I. Large and small formal units.
   A. Phrases and periods, if any; phrase-groups; extensions and elisions.
   B. Overall form, including large letters for main sections and formal label if appropriate. Note balance and proportion of sections.
   C. Use of repetition, altered repetition, departure, return, altered return, development, and contrast. Note use of developmental devices.
   D. Elements of unity versus elements of variety.
   E. Stable versus unstable areas (tension versus relaxation).

II. Melodic organization.
   A. Motivic structure, both melodic and rhythmic.
   B. Melodic structure, including departure note and goal note, contour, climax, main structural pitches, range, and tessitura.
   C. Special aspects, such as contrapuntal devices and sequence.

III. Rhythmic organization.
   A. Surface rhythm, meter, harmonic rhythm.
   B. Special devices of rhythmic development.
   C. How is the meter emphasized or obscured?
   D. Tempo.

IV. Harmonic language.
   A. All keys and chords, with Roman numerals and figured bass symbols, or appropriate contemporary nomenclature. How are the key and mode established?
   B. All modulations, indicating type and placement.
   C. All cadences, indicating type and placement.
   D. All nonharmonic tones, by type.
   E. Functional and nonfunctional use of chromaticism.
   F. Use of nonfunctional (linear, coloristic) chords.

V. Sound.
   A. Use of the medium: idiomatic devices, range and tessitura, timbre (color).
   B. Texture.
   C. Dynamics.

VI. Text setting, where appropriate.
   A. Relations between form and/or mood of text and music.
   B. Rhythmic and/or metric relationships.

* Additional model analyses may be found on pages 11, 27, 119, 204, 234, 264, 402, and 418.

ADDITIONAL QUESTIONS
FOR THE ANALYSIS OF TWENTIETH-CENTURY MUSIC

  I. Tonal centers, if any.
     A. How are they established?
     B. Do they change?
  II. Scalar materials.
     A. What type or types are employed?
     B. Do they change or are they inflected?
 III. Harmonic vocabulary.
     A. What types of chord structures are used?
     B. Is chord succession systematic? If so, how?
 IV. Special metric and rhythmic characteristics.
  V. Refer to pages 401–403 for more comments and questions.

Sample Analysis

Mozart, *Symphony in G Minor*, K. 550

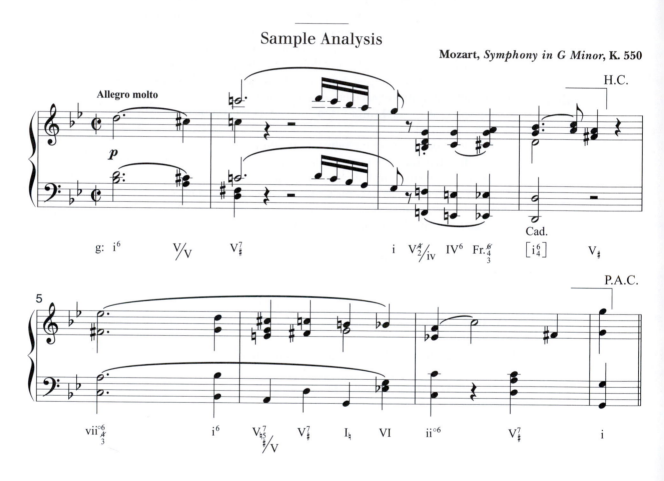

Observations:

A. Form: sequential (or similar) period. Two four-measure phrases, with a half cadence in m. 4, and a perfect authentic cadence in m. 8.

B. Motivic coherence: there appears on the surface to be a good deal of motivic material, but on closer examination the principal melodic gesture is a series of decending chromatic lines in the upper and bass voices.

C. Counterpoint: the bass and tenor lines in mm. 3-4 form a typical chromatic contrary motion approach to the half cadence.

D. Rhythm: the surface rhythm is somewhat irregular and slower at the beginnings of each phase, then accelerates toward the cadences.

E. Harmonic Rhythm: the harmonic rhythm also varies, with both phrases accelerating.

F. Melodic Structure

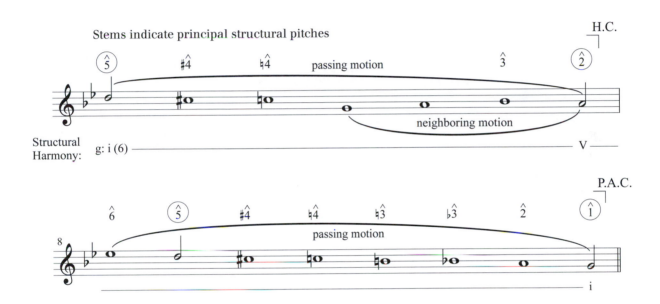

Appendix B

For Further Reference

Aldwell, Edward, and Carl Schachter. *Harmony and Voice Leading,* 3rd ed. Belmont, CA: Thomson/Schirmer, 2003.

Benjamin, Thomas, Michael Horvit, and Robert Nelson. *Techniques and Materials of Music.* 7th ed. Belmont, CA: Thomson/Schirmer, 2008.

Benjamin, Thomas. *The Craft of Tonal Counterpoint,* 2nd ed. New York: Routledge, 2003.

Benward, Bruce, and Gary White. *Music in Theory and Practice,* 7th ed. New York: McGraw-Hill, 2003.

Berry, Wallace. *Form in Music,* 2nd ed. Englewood Cliffs, NJ: Prentice-Hall, 1985.

Clendinning, Jane Piper, and Elizabeth West Marvin. *The Musician's Guide to Theory and Analysis.* New York: W.W. Norton, 2005.

Dallin, Leon. *Twentieth Century Composition,* 3rd ed. Dubuque, IA: William C. Brown, 1974.

Forte, Allen. *The Structure of Atonal Music.* New Haven, CT: Yale University Press, 1977.

Gauldin, Robert. *Harmonic Practice in Tonal Music,* 2nd Ed. New York: Norton, 2004.

Gauldin, Robert. *A Practical Approach to Eighteenth-Century Counterpoint.* Prospect Heights, IL: Waveland Press, 1995.

Henry, Earl, and Michael Rogers. *Tonality and Design in Music Theory.* Upper Saddle River, NJ: Pearson/Prentice Hall, 2005.

Kennan, Kent. *Counterpoint: Based on Eighteenth Century Practice,* 4th ed. Englewood Cliffs, NJ: Prentice-Hall, 1998.

Kostka, Stefan. *Materials and Techniques of Twentieth-Century Music.* 3rd ed. Englewood Cliffs, NJ: Prentice-Hall, 2005.

Kostka, Stefan, and Dorothy Payne. *Tonal Harmony, with an Introduction to Twentieth Century Music,* 5th ed. Boston: McGraw-Hill, 2004.

Laitz, Stephen G. *The Complete Musician: An Integrated Approach to Tonal Theory, Listening, and Analysis,* 2nd ed. New York: Oxford University Press, 2004.

Lester, Joel. *Analytic Approach to Twentieth-Century Music.* New York: Norton, 1989.

Ottman, Robert W. *Elementary Harmony,* 5th ed. Englwood Cliffs, NJ: Prentice-Hall, 1998

____*Advanced Harmony,* 5th ed. Englewood Cliffs, NJ: Prentice-Hall, 2000.

Persichetti, Vincent. *Twentieth-Century Harmony.* New York: Norton, 1961.

Piston, Walter. *Harmony,* 5th ed. Revised and expanded by Mark De Voto. New York: Norton, 1987.

Roig-Francoli, Miguel. *Harmony in Context.* Boston: McGraw-Hill, 2003.

Spencer, Peter, and Peter M. Temko. *A Practical Approach to the Study of Form in Music.* Prospect Heights, IL: Waveland Press, 1994.

Steinke, Greg. *Bridge to 20th-Century Music.* Boston: Allyn and Bacon, 1999.

Strauss, Joseph. *Introduction to Post-Tonal Theory,* 3rd ed. Englewood Cliffs, NJ: Prentice-Hall, 2005.

Appendix C

Textbook Correlation Chart

ALDWELL/SCHACHTER 3rd Edition		BENJAMIN 7th Edition	BENWARD 7th Edition	CLENDINNING 2005	GAULDIN 2nd Edition
Chapter	Chapter	Part.Chapter	Volume.Chapter	Chapter	Chapter
1	6	II.2	1.4	7,12	9
2	6	II.3	1.4	7,12	9
3	8	II.4, III.7	1.11, 2.10	7,12	10,35
4	9	II.5,6,7	1.2	7	9
5	10	II.8	1.9	15	16
6	7, 11	II.9	1.2, 1.4, 1.9	7	11,13
7	9	II.10	1.2	7	14
8	8	II.11	1.9, 1.11	7	13
9	19	II.12	1.9	15	16
10	11, 15	II.13	1.2	16	17
11	15	II.14	1.4	7	13
12	17, 23	II.15	2.4	24	28
13	12	II.17	1.13	7	14
14	22	II.18	1.12	7	19
15	24	II.19	1.13	7	19
17	25	III.1	1.15	19, 21	21
18	26	III.2	1.14	22	22
20	25	III.3	2.13	29	32
21	28	III.4	2.5	25	29
22	29	III.5	2.6	25	30
23	29	III.5		25	30
24	29, 30	III.5	2.6	25	30
25	26, 31	III.6	2.13	24	34,40
26	27	III.7	2.10	26	35
27	31	IV.4	2.1		37,39
29		V.19	2.2, 2.3	8,9,11	App. 3
30	27, 31	IV.4	2.12	26	App. 4
31	1	IV.5	2.1	30	App. 2
32	31	IV.6	2.15		
33	31	IV.7	2.14	30	App. 2
34		IV.8	2.14, 2.15		
35		IV.9	2.15		
36		IV.10	2.15	30-32	42
37		IV.11	2.Postlude	33-34	
38		IV.1,12	2.Postlude	36,37	

(cont'd)

Note: Units containing complete pieces are not listed in the Correlation Chart since, by definition, they are comprehensive and cumulative and will illustrate all the techniques and materials discussed in specific units to that point.

Textbook Correlation Chart

Chapter	HENRY/ROGERS 2005 I.Ch or II.Ch	KOSTKA 4th Edition Chapter	KOSTKA 5th Edition Chapter	LAITZ 2nd Edition Chapter	OTTMAN 5th Edition E.Ch or A.Ch	PISTON 5th Edition Chapter	ROIG-FRANCOLI 2003 Chapter
1	I.3,5	4,7	4,7	5	E.3,4	2,3,4	F,2
2	I.3,5	4,7	4,7	5	E.3,4	2,3,4,5	F,2
3	I.3,5	4,26,28	4,26	5,6,9	3.13,A.10	15	F,12
4	I.3,5	4,7	4,7	12,14	E.6	2,3,4,5,13	F,3
5	I.8	9	9	14	E.9	10	9
6	I.3	8	8	10, 14	E.9	6	4
7	I.3	4,7	4,7	12	E.10	2,3,4,5	10
8	I.3,5	13	13	11	E.13	15	12
9	I.8	9	9	14	E.9	10	9
10	I.3	4,7	4,7	18, 19	E.14	2,3,4,5	14
11	I.3,5	4,7,8	4,7,8	10	E.10	2,6	13
12	I.11	21	21	27,28	A.7	4,5	22
13	I.8	14	14	17	E.13	23	15
14	I.8	14	14	11	A.2	23	15
15	I.8	15	15	6,23	A.6	23	15
17	I.10	16	16	24	E.18	16,17	16,17
18	I.11	18, 19	18,19	25	E.18,A.1	14,20	19
20	I.9,10	26	26	11,24	A.2,3	21	18
21	II.4	22	22	29	A.7	26	23
22	II.3,4	23	23	30	A.8,9	27,28	23
23	II.4	24	24	30	A.8,9	27,28	23
24	II.4	24	24	30	A.8,9	27,28	23
25	II.4	25	25	28	A.11	14,21,26,27	24,25
26	II.7	26	26		A.10	24	27
27	II.7,8	26	26	25	A.10	24	27
29	II.2	27	27	4		8,19, 29	G,21
30	II.9	27	28	35	A.10	31	27
31	II.8	21	28		E.AppD,A.13	5,30	C
32	II.8	28	28		A.15	31	29
33	II.8	28	28		A.13	31	C,30
34	I.3,II.8	28	28		A.13	31	30
35	II.9	28	28		A.15	31	29
36	II.10	28	28		A.16	32	29
37	II.11	28	28		A.16	32	29,30
38	II.12	28	28		A.16		15,22,23,27

ACKNOWLEDGMENTS

Unit 13   *Blue Moon* by Richard Rodgers and Lorenz Hart. © 1934 (Renewed) Metro-Goldwyn-Mayer Inc. All Rights controlled by EMI Robbins Catalog Inc. All Rights Reserved. Excerpt used by Permission of Alfred Publishing Company, Inc., Van Nuys, CA 91410.

Unit 19   *I Got Rhythm* music and lyrics by George Gershwin and Ira Gershwin. © 1930 (Renewed) WB Music Corp. All Rights Reserved. Gershwin ® and George Gershwin ® are registered trademarks of Gershwin Enterprises. Used by permission of Alfred Publishing Co., Inc.

Unit 20   *The Girl Friend* by Richard Rodgers and Lorenz Hart. © 1926 (Renewed) Warner Bos. Inc. Rights for Extended Renewal Term in the U.S. controlled by The Estate of Lorenz Hart (administered by WB Music Corp.) and The Family Trust U/W Richard Rodgers and The Family Trust U/W Dorothy F. Rodgers (administered by Williamson Music). All Rights Reserved. Excerpt used by Permission of Alfred Publishing Company, Inc., Van Nuys, CA 91410.

Unit 30   *Symphony No. 2,* Op. 30 (excerpt), by Howard Hanson. Copyright © 1932 by the Eastman School of Music. Copyright renewed. All Rights Reserved. Reprinted by permission Carl Fischer, LLC.

Mysterious Mountain, I, Andante (excerpt), by Alan Hovhaness. Copyright © 1944 (Renewed) by Associated Music Publishers, Inc. (BMI). International Copyright Secured. All Rights Reserved. Reprinted by Permission of G. Schimer, Inc.

Slaughter on Tenth Avenue music by Richard Rogers. © 1936 (Renewed) Williamson Music, Inc. All Rights Administered by WB Music Corp. (Publishing) and Alfred Publishing Co., Inc. (Print). All Rights Reserved.

Prelude to a Kiss words by Irving Mills and Irving Gordon, music by Duke Ellington. © 1938 (Renewed) EMI Mills Music, Inc., and Famous Music Corporation in the USA. All Rights outside the USA Controlled by EMI Mills Music, Inc. (Publishing) and Alfred Publishing Co., Inc. (Print). All Rights Reserved.

Jordu by Duke Jordan. Copyright © Slow Dancing Music and Tamara Shad, 3060 Deep Canyon Drive, Beverly Hills, CA 90210. Used by permission. All rights reserved.

Laura lyrics by Johnny Mercer, music by David Raksin. © 1945 (Renewed) by Twentieth Century Music Corporation. All Rights Controlled by EMI Robbins Catalog, Inc. (Publishing) and Alfred Publishing Co., Inc. (Print). All Rights Reserved.

Unit 31   *Ten Preludes for the Piano*, No. 1 (excerpt), by Carlos Chavez. Copyright © 1940 (Renewed) by G. Schirmer, Inc. (ASCAP). International Copyright Secured. All Rights Reserved. Reprinted by Permission.

Valse (excerpt) by Francis Poulenc. Copyright © 1920 Editions Max Eschig. Used by Permission of Theodore Presser Company.

Ceremony of Carols, No. 8, by Benjamin Britten. © Copyright 1943 by Boosey & Co., Ltd. Copyright renewed. Reprinted by permission of Boosey & Hawkes, Inc.

Susannah, Act II, Scene 3, "The Trees on the Mountain" (excerpt) by Carlisle Floyd. Copyright © 1956, 1957 Boosey & Hawkes, Inc. Copyright Renewed. Reprinted by permission.

Fourteen Bagatelles, Op. 6, No. 4 (excerpt), by Bela Bartók. Copyright © 1908 by Editio Musica Budapest. Copyright Renewed. Reprinted by permission of Boosey & Hawkes, Inc., U.S. Agent.

Work Song by Nat Adderley. Copyright © 1960, Renewed 1988 by Upam Music Co., a division of Gopam Enterprises, Inc. All rights reserved. Used by permission.

Blue Rondo à La Turk (excerpt) by Dave Brubeck. © Copyright 1960 (renewed 1988) Derry Music Company, San Francisco, California. Used with Permission. All Rights Reserved.

Unit 35   *Symphony No. 5,* I (excerpt), by Arthur Honegger. Copyright © 1951 Éditions Salabert. Reprinted by permission.

A Three Score Set, II (excerpt), by William Schuman. Copyright © 1944 (Renewed) by Associated Music Publishers, Inc. (BMI). International Copyright Secured. All Rights Reserved. Reprinted by Permission of G. Schirmer, Inc.

Allegro Giocoso (excerpt) by Leo Kraft. Copyright © Lawson-Gould Music Publishers, Warner Bros. Publications.

The Rake's Progress, "Prelude," by Igor Stravinsky. © Copyright 1949, 1950, 1951 by Boosey & Hawkes, Inc. Boosey & Hawkes, Inc.

44 Duos, No. 33 (excerpt) by Bela Bartók. © Copyright 1933 for the USA by Boosey & Hawkes, Inc. Copyright Renewed. Reprinted by permission of Boosey & Hawkes, Inc.

Strange Meadowlark (excerpt) by Dave Brubeck. Copyright © 1960 (renewed 1988) Derry Music Company, San Francisco, California. Used with Permission. All Rights Reserved.

Unit 36   *Drei Klavierstücke,* Op. 11, No. 1 (excerpt) by Arnold Schonberg. Used by permission of Belmont Music Publishers.

Klavierstücke, Op. 19, No. 2 (excerpt) by Arnold Schönberg. Used by permission of Belmont Music Publishers.

Pierrot Lunaire, Op. 21, No. 7, "Mondestrunken," by Arnold Schönberg. Used by permission of Belmont Music Publishers.

Five Movements for String Quartet, Op. 5, No. 4, by Anton Webern. © 1922 by Universal Edition. © renewed. All Rights Reserved. Used by permission of European American Music Distributors LLC, U.S. and Canadian agent for Universal Edition A.G., Wien.

Mikrokosmos, No. 144, "Minor Seconds, Major Sevenths" (excerpt), by Bela Bartók. © Copyright 1940 by Hawkes & Son (London) Ltd. Copyright Renewed. Definitive corrected edition © Copyright 1987 by Hawkes & Son (London) Ltd. Reprinted by permission of Boosey & Hawkes, Inc.

String Quartet No. 4, I (excerpt) by Bela Bartók. © Copyright 1928 for the USA by Boosey & Hawkes, Inc. Copyright Renewed. Reprinted by Permission.

Two Episodes, No. 1, by Arthur Berger. Copyright © Lawson-Gould Music Publishers. Warner Bros. Publications.

Unit 37   *Three Impressions in the Twelve-Tone Technique,* "Dancing Toys," by Ernst Krenek. Copyright © 1939 (Renewed) by G. Schirmer, Inc. (ASCAP). International Copyright Secured. All Rights Reserved. Reprinted by Permission.

Suite für Klavier, Op. 25, "Gavotte" by Arnold Schönberg. Used by permission of Belmont Music Publishers.

Cinque Frammenti di Saffo by Luigi Dallapiccola. © Copyright 1943 by Edizione Suivini Zerboni S.P.A. Reprinted by permission of Sugar-Melodi Inc.

Drei Lieder, op. 25, No. 1, by Anton Webern. © 1956 by Universal Edition A.G., Wien. © renewed. All Rights Reserved. Used by permission of European American Music Distributors LLC, U.S. and Canadian agent for Universal Edition A.G., Wien.

Unit 38   *Klavierstücke,* No. 2 (excerpt) by Karlheinz Stockhausen. © 1954 by Universal Edition (London) Ltd., London. © renewed. All Rights Reserved. Used by permission of European American Music Distributors LLC, U.S. and Canadian agent for Universal Edition A.G., Wien.

String Quartet (excerpt) by Witold Lutoslawski. Copyright © 1967, 1993 Chester Music Limited for the world except Poland, Albania, Bulgaria, the territories of former Czechoslovakia, Romania, Hungary, and the whole territory of the former USSR, Cuba, China, Vietnam, and North Korea, where the copyright is held by Polskie Wydawnictwo Muzyczne, Krakow, Poland. International Copyright Secured. All Rights Reserved. Reprinted by Permission G. Schirmer, Inc. U.S. Agent.

String Quartet No. 2 (excerpt) by Krzysztof Penderecki. © 1961 (Renewed) EMI Deshon Music, Inc. and PWM Editions. All Rights Reserved. Excerpt used by Permission of Warner Bros. Publications U.S. Inc., Miami, FL, 33014.

Madrigals, Book IV, No. 2, by George Crumb. © 1971 by C. F. Peters Corporation. Used by permission.

Index of Composers and Their Compositions

(Numbers in **bold** refer to *selection* numbers.)

Adderly, Nathaniel (1931–2000)
Work Song **400**
Bach, Johann Christoff Friedrich (1732–1795)
Menuet **97** Track 10
Nun danket alle Gott **59** Track 8
Bach, Johann Sebastian (1685–1750)
Ach Gott, vom Himmel sieh' darein **259** Track 59
Aus meines Herzens Grunde **105** Track 11
Cantata No. 4: Sinfonia **366**
Christ lag in Todesbanden **233**
Christmas Oratorio, no. 4: Introduction **199**
Chorale Prelude on "Christ lag in Todesbanden" **368**
Chorale Prelude on "In Dulci Jubilo" **367**
Ein' feste Burg ist unser Gott **348**
Es ist genug, so nimm, Herr **349**
French Suite in C minor **230** Track 47
French Suite in D minor **164** Track 21
Herr, ich habe mißgehandelt **112**
Ich hab' mein' Sach' Gott heimgestellt **270**
In dulci jubilo **232** Track 49
Invention No. 4, BWV 775 **371**
Invention No. 13 **260, 372** Track 60
Lobt Gott, ihr Christen, allzugleich **39** Track 6
O Ewigkeit, du Donnerwort **157** Track 19
Schmücke dich, o liebe Seele **87** Track 10
Sinfonia 3, BWV 789 **373**
St. Matthew Passion, no. 78 **332**
Straf' mich nicht in deinem Zorn **130**
The Well-Tempered Clavier, Vol. I, Fugue 2 **374**
The Well-Tempered Clavier, Vol. II, Fugue 9 **375**
The Well-Tempered Clavier, Vol. II, Fugue 17 **268**
Wachet auf, ruft uns die Stimme **231** Track 48

Wer nur den lieben Gott läßt walten **284**
Barber, Samuel (1910–1981)
Excursions, III **405**
Bartók, Béla (1887–1945)
Concerto for Orchestra **424**
Fourteen Bagatelles, op. 6, no. 4 **398**
Fourteen Bagatelles, op. 6, no. 6 **419**
Fourteen Bagatelles, op. 6, no. 10 **415**
Forty-Four Violin Duets, no. 33 **437**
Fourth String Quartet **444**
Little Pieces for Children, no. III **389**
Mikrokosmos, no. 78: Five Tone Scale **409**
Mikrokosmos, no. 107: Melody in the Mist **426**
Mikrokosmos, no. 101: Diminished Fifth **417**
Mikrokosmos, no. 136: Whole Tone Scale **413**
Mikrokosmos, no. 144: Minor Seconds, Major Sevenths **443**
Sketches, op. 9, no. 6 **418**
Beach, Amy (1867–1944)
Phantoms **361**
Beethoven, Ludwig von (1770–1827)
Bagatelle, op. 119, no. 1 **271** Track 64
Concerto No. 1 for Piano, op. 15 **69**
Contradanse **80, 245** Track 9, Track 55
Coriolan Overture, op. 62 **272**
Egmont Overture, op. 84 **29**
Fidelio, Act I, no. 9 **45**
Für Elise **12** Track 2
Leonora Overture No. 2, op. 72 **3**
Minuet **165** Track 22
Minuet in C **68** Track 8
Quartet, op. 18, no. 2 **228**; no. 3 **247, 266**; no. 6 **347**
Quintet, op. 29 **189**
Scottish Dance **168** Track 25
Seven Country Dances, no. 7 **33**
Sieben Variationen, **359**
Six Variations on "Nel cor più non mi sento" **52** Track 7

561

Beethoven, Ludwig von, *continued*

Sonata, op. 2, no. 3 **365**

Sonata, op. 13 **317** Track 81

Sonata, op. 14, no. 2 **138** Track 13

Sonata, op. 26 **235** Track 57

Sonata, op. 31, no. 3 **63** Track 8

Sonata, op. 53 **193** Track 32

Sonata, op. 109 **277** Track 67

Sonata in F major **239** Track 54

Sonatina in G major **76, 177** Track 9

(I, m. 25), Track 29 (II)

String Quartet, op. 59, no. 2 **264**

Symphony No. 1, op. 21 **181, 275**

Symphony No. 2, op. 36 **67, 137, 208**

Symphony No. 3, op. 55 **82**

Symphony No. 4, op. 60 **21, 184**

Symphony No. 5, op. 67 **8, 15, 44, 127, 311**

Symphony No. 6, op. 68 **133, 139**

Symphony No. 7, op. 92 **77, 222, 243, 315**

Theme from Six Easy

Variations **328** Track 84

Thirty-Two Variations,

Var. 30 **279** Track 68

Trio, op. 1, no. 1 **173, 179**; no. 3 **95, 195**

Trio, op. 11 **190, 323**

Trio, op. 70, no. 1 **318**

Trio, op. 70, no. 2 **5**

Trio, op. 97 **38**

Trio, op. 121A **55**

Bellini, Vincenzo (1801–1835)

I Puritani, Act II, scene 3 **253**

Berg, Alban (1885–1935)

Four Songs, op. 2, no. 3 **387**

Wozzeck, Act II **425, 427**

Berger, Arthur (1912–2003)

Two Episodes, I **445**

Bizet, Georges (1838–1875)

Carmen, Act II, Entr'acte **140**

Bononcini, Giovanni (1670–1747)

Deh più a me non vàscondete **225**

Brahms, Johannes (1833–1897)

Ballade, op. 10, no. 4 **145** Track 16

Chorale Prelude on Oh wie selig seid

ihr doch, ihr Frommen **369**

Der Tod, das ist die kühle Nacht,

op. 96, no. 1 **340**

Intermezzo, op. 76,

no. 4 **300** Track 75

Intermezzo in A major, op. 118,

no. 2 **262** Track 61

Liebeslieder Walzer, op. 52,

no. 4 **256**

Quintet, op. 115 **221**

Romance, op. 118, no. 5 **100** Track 10

Symphony No. 3, op. 90 **125**

Symphony No. 4, op. 98 **92, 128**

Variations on a Theme by Handel,

var. 20 **342** Track 91

Waltz, op. 39 **237** Track 52;

no. 15 **227** Track 46

Wenn du nur zuweilen lächelst,

op. 57, no. 2 **310**

Wie bist du meine Königen, op. 32,

no. 9 **321**

Wie Melodien zieht es mir, op. 105 **265**

Britten, Benjamin (1913–1976)

Ceremony of Carols, no. 8 **394**

Brubeck, Dave (1920–)

Blue Rondo à la Turk **430**

Strange Meadowlark **438**

Buxtehude, Dietrich (1637–1707)

Passacaglia **81**

Byrd, William (1543–1623)

Pavana "The Earle of Salisbury" **115**

Casella, Alfredo (1883–1947)

Siciliana **399**

Chávez, Carlos (1899–1978)

Ten Preludes, no. 1 **390**

Chopin, Frédéric (1810–1849)

Mazurka, op. 6, no. 1 **339** Track 90

Mazurka, op. 7, no. 2 **213** Track 40

Mazurka, op. 17, no. 1 **28** Track 4

Mazurka, op. 24, no. 3 **36**

Mazurka, op. 33, no. 2 **57** Track 7

Mazurka, op. 67, no. 2 **201**

Mazurka, op. post 67,

no. 2 **353** Track 33

Polens Grabgesang, op. 74 **6**

Prelude, op. 28, no. 6 **269** Track 63;

no. 9 **347** Track 92; no. 15 **331**

Track 86; no. 20 **263**

Track 62; no. 22 **302** Track 77

Valse, op. 69, no. 1 **202** Track 34

Valse Brillante, op. 34, no. 1 **329**

Track 85; no. 3 **203** Track 35

Valse (Posthumous) **7** Track 1

Zwei Leichen **54**

Copland, Aaron (1900–1990)

The Young Pioneers **404**

Corelli, Arcangelo (1653–1713)

Sonata for Violin and Continuo, op. 5,

no. 9 **93**

Couperin, François (1668–1733)

Carnival **9**

Le Petit Rien **48** Track 6

(Numbers in **bold** refer to *selection* numbers.)

Cowell, Henry (1897–1965)
   The Irishman Dances **403**
   Tiger **428**
Crüger, Johann (1598–1662)
   Herzliebster Jesu, was hast du
      verbrochen **85** ⊕ Track 10
Crumb, George (1929–   )
   Madrigals, Book IV **453**
Czerny, Carl (1791–1857)
   Sonatina, op. 792, no. 8 **2** ⊕ Track 1

Dallapiccola, Luigi (1904–1975)
   Cinque Frammenti di Saffo **448**
Dandrieu, Jean (1682–1738)
   Les Fifres **49**
Daquin, Louis-Claude (1694–1772)
   La Joyeuse **111**
Debussy, Claude (1862–1918)
   Pelléas et Mélisande, Act I,
      scene 1 **381**;
   Pelléas et Mélisande, Act II,
      scene I **414**
   Pour le Piano: Sarabande **458**
      ⊕ Track 98
   Préludes, II: Voiles **412** ⊕ Track 97;
      X: La Cathédrale
      engloutie **459** ⊕ Track 99
   Suite bergamasque, Passepied **395**
   Trois Chansons, no. 1 **392**
Donizetti, Gaetano (1797–1848)
   Linda di Chamounix, "O Luce di
      quest'anima" **120**
   Lucia di Lammermoor, Act I,
      Cavatina **220**; Act II, no. 6 **37**
Druckman, Jacob (1928–   )
   Valentine, for solo contrabass **454**
Dvôrák, Antonin (1841–1904)
   Quartet, op. 96 **142**

Ellington, Edward "Duke" (1889–1972)
   Prelude to a Kiss **385**

Fauré, Gabriel (1845–1924)
   Après un Rêve **338**
Floyd, Carlisle (1926–   )
   Susannah, Act II, scene 3 **396**
Franck, César (1822–1890)
   Sonata for Violin and Piano **327**
   Symphony in D minor **343**

Gershwin, George (1898–1937)
   I Got Rhythm **241**
   Porgy and Bess, "Summertime" **467**
   Someone to Watch Over Me **204**

Gluck, Christoph Willibald (1714–1787)
   Orphée, Act I, no. 1 **153**;
      nos. 6 and 7 **295**
Gounod, Charles (1818–1893)
   Faust, Act I, no. 6 **83**; Act IV,
      no. 18 **249**
Granados, Enrique (1867–1916)
   Valses Poeticos **292** ⊕ Track 72
Grieg, Edvard Haggerup (1843–1907)
   Alfedans, op. 12 **288** ⊕ Track 70
   Erotikon **355** ⊕ Track 94
   Grandmother's Minuet, op. 68,
      no. 2 **334** ⊕ Track 87
   Norsk **172**
   Solvejg's Lied **308** ⊕ Track 79
   Voegtersang **132** ⊕ Track 13
   Wedding Day at Troldhaugen, op. 65,
      no. 6 **336** ⊕ Track 89

Handel, George Frederick (1685–1759)
   Aria con Variazioni, Leçon No. 1 **154**
   Courante **107**
   Judas Maccabaeus, Part III, No. 53,
      Introduction **151**
   Menuet, Leçon
      No. 2 **162, 234** ⊕ Track 50
   Prelude **238** ⊕ Track 53
   Sonata for Flute and
      Continuo **146, 161**
   Sonata for Flute and Continuo **90**
   Sonata for Flute and Continuo **200**
   Suite XI **182** ⊕ Track 31
   Suite XVI **192**
Hanson, Howard (1896–1981)
   Symphony No. 2, op. 30 **377**
Haydn, Franz Joseph (1732–1809)
   Haydn (?) Allegro **147**
      ⊕ Track 17
   Minuet **209** ⊕ Track 38
   Quartet, op. 3, no. 5 **72**
   Sonata in A♭ major, Hob. XVI: 46 **131**
   Sonata in C major, Hob. XVI:
      35 **60** ⊕ Track 8
   Sonata in C♯ minor, Hob. XVI:
      36 **211** ⊕ Track 39
   Sonata in D major, Hob. XVI: 4 **109**;
      37 **42, 79** ⊕ Track 6 (III, m. 114),
      Track 9
   Sonata in E major,
      Hob. XVI: 13 **20** ⊕ Track 3
   Sonata in E♭ major,
      Hob. XVI: 49 **108** ⊕ Track 11
   Sonata in E minor,
      Hob. XVI: 34 **58, 218** ⊕ Track 43

Haydn, Franz Joseph, *continued*
    Sonata in G major, Hob. XVI: 27 **240**;
        39 **214**   Track 41
    Sonatina,
        Hob. XVI: 1 **224**   Track 45
    Sonatina in C major,
        Hob. XVI: 7 **122**
         Track 12
    Sonatina in D major, Hob. XVI: 4 **109**
    Sonatina in G major, Hob. XVI: 8 **1**
        11 **150**   Track 18
    String Quartet, op. 76, no. 6 **316**
    Symphony No. 104, Hob. I: 104, Menuet
        223, 242, 254
    Trio, Hob. XV: 25 **278**
    Trio in C major, Hob. XV: 3 **65**
    Trio in D major **176**
    Trio in F♯ minor, Hob. XV: 26 **217**
    Trio in G major, Hob. XV: 25 **148**
Herbert, Victor (1859–1924)
    Gypsy Love Song **289**
Hindemith, Paul (1895–1963)
    Ludus Tonalis, Fuga secunda
        in G **423**; Fuga undecima
        in B (Canon) **463**
    Mathis der Maler: Grablegung **420**
    Piano Sonata No. 2, I **469**
Honegger, Artur (1892–1955)
    Symphony No. 5 **431**
Horne, David (1970–   )
    Six Short Studies, Sixteenth Notes **456**
Hovhaness, Alan (1911–2000)
    Mysterious Mountain **379**

Ives, Charles (1874–1954)
    Majority **421, 429**

Joplin, Scott (1868–1917)
    A Breeze from Alabama **362**
Jordan, Duke (1922–   )
    Jordu **388**

Kabalevsky, Dmitri (1904–   )
    Sonatina, op. 13 **378**
    Toccatina **393**
Kern, Jerome (1885–1945)
    Can I Forget You? **206**
    Look for the Silver Lining **32**
Kodály, Zoltán (1882–1967)
    Valsette **410**
Kraft, Leo (1922–1991)
    Allegro Giocoso **433**

Krenek, Ernst (1900–   )
    Dancing Toys, op. 83, no. 1 **446**
    Piano Piece, op. 39, no. 5 **422**
Kuhlau, Friederich (1786–1832)
    Sonatina, op. 20, no. 1 **66**   Track 8
    Sonatina, op. 88, no. 3 **74**   Track 9
Kuhnau, Johann (1660–1722)
    Biblical Sonata No. 1: Victory Dance
        and Festival **11**   Track 2

Liszt, Franz (1811–1886)
    Il pensieroso, from Années de
        Pèlerinage **356**   Track 95
    Les Préludes **244**
    Liebestraum, no. 3 **306**   Track 78
Lutoslawski, Witold (1915–1994)
    Bucolic, no. 3 **416**
    String Quartet (1965) **451**

Macmillan, James (1959–   )
    Piano Sonata, I **470**
Mattheson, Johann (1681–1764)
    Minuet **117**   Track 12
Mendelssohn, Felix (1809–1847)
    Elijah, op. 70, no. 1 **282**; no. 29 **29**
    Fugue no. 2, op. 35 **376**
    Kinderstück, op. 72,
        no. 1 **159**   Track 20
    Lieder ohne Wörte, op. 30,
        no. 3 **352**   Track 93
    Midsummer Night's Dream, op. 61:
        Overture **337**
    Midsummer Night's Dream, op. 61:
        Wedding March **197**
Milhaud, Darius (1892–1974)
    Saudades do Brazil, no. 6: Gavea, **460**
        no. 7: Corcovado **436**
    Touches Blanches **402**
    Touches Noires **408**
Moussorgsky, Modest (1839–1881)
    Songs and Dances of Death, no. 4 **294**
Mozart, Wolfgang Amadeus (1756–1791)
    Abendempfindung, K. 523 **43**
    Adagio **291**   Track 71
    Bastien und Bastienne, K. 46B, no. 1 **88**
        no. 9 **40**
    Concerto in A major,
        K. 488 **257**   Track 58
    Die Entführung aus dem Serail, K. 384,
        Act III, no. 18 **313**
    Die Zauberflöte, K. 620, Act II, no. 21 **53**
    Minuet, K. 355 **350**

(Numbers in **bold** refer to *selection* numbers.)

Quartet, K. 464 **62**

Requiem, K. 626, Offertorium **149**

Rondo **10** ⊙ Track 2

Rondo, K. 485 **71** ⊙ Track 9

Rondo, K. 494 **158**

Sonata, K. 280 **110** ⊙ Track 11

Sonata, K. 281 **174** ⊙ Track 27

Sonata, K. 282,
　　Menuet I **215** ⊙ Track 42

Sonata, K. 283 **96** ⊙ Track 10

Sonata, K. 309 **364**

Sonata, K. 310 **118, 135** ⊙ Track 12
　　(III, m. 211), Track 13 (I m. 129)

Sonata, K. 330 **219** ⊙ Track 44

Sonata, K. 331 **207** ⊙ Track 37

Sonata, K. 332 **17, 41** ⊙ Track 3
　　(III, m. 15), Track 6 (I, m. 145)

Sonata, K. 457 **143, 276** ⊙ Track 14,
　　Track 66 (III, m.167)

Sonata, K. 545 **89** ⊙ Track 10

Sonata, K. 570 **46** ⊙ Track 6

Sonata for Violin and Piano,
　　K. 306 **121, 156**

Symphony No. 35, K. 385 **75**

Symphony No. 39, K. 543 **206**

Symphony No. 40, K. 550 **360**

Symphony No. 41, K. 551 **78, 212**

Valse **25**

Waltz, K. 567 **251** ⊙ Track 57

Pachelbel, Johann (1653–1706)

　Chaconne **113**

　Fantasie **160**

Paisiello, Giovanni (1740–1816)

　Le donne sur balcone **61**

Penderecki, Krzystof (1933–　　)

　String Quartet, no. 2 **452**

Porter, Cole (1891–1964)

　Night and Day **466**

Poulenc, Francis (1899–1963)

　Gloria, Laudamus te **407**

　Valse **391**

Prokofiev, Sergei (1891–1953)

　Classical Symphony, op. 25 **461**

　March from The Love of
　　Three Oranges **462**

Purcell, Henry (c. 1659–1695)

　Dido and Aeneas, Act I, scene I **229**

　Dido and Aeneas, Thy Hand Belinda **370**

　Rigadoon **169**

Rachmaninoff, Sergei (1873–1943)

　Melodie, op. 3, no. 3 **324**

Rameau, Jean-Philippe (1682–1764)

　Minuet **170**

　Sarabande I, vol. I **64**

Raksin, David (1912–2004) Laura **388**

Ravel, Maurice (1875–1937)

　Mother Goose Suite:
　　The Magic Garden **401**

　Sonatine, Mouv^t II **457**

　Valses Nobles et Sentimentales **383**

Rimsky-Korsakov, Nicolai (1844–1908)

　Le Coq d'Or: Hymn to the Sun **4**

　Snowmaiden, Chanson du Bonhomme
　　Hiver **307**

Rodgers, Richard (1902–1980)

　Blue Moon **141**

　The Girl Friend **255**

　Slaughter on Tenth Avenue **384**

Rouse, Christopher (1949–　　)

　Valentine **455**

Ruggles, Carl (1876–1971)

　Evocations, no. 1 **464**

Saint-Saëns, Camille (1835–1921)

　Carneval des Animaux,
　　Le Cygne **226**

Scarlatti, Alessandro (1660–1725)

　Folia **116** ⊙ Track 12

Scheidt, Samuel (1587–1654)

　Bergamasca **26** ⊙ Track 4

Schönberg, Arnold (1874–1951)

　Drei Klavierstücke, op. 11, no. 1 **439**

　Klavierstücke, op. 19, no. 2 **440**

　Pierrot Lunaire, op. 21, no. 1:
　　Mondestrunken **441**

　Suite für Klavier, op. 25: Gavotte **447**;
　　Menuett **465**

Schubert, Franz (1797–1828)

　Aufenthalt **123**

　Dance **166** ⊙ Track 23

　Der Müller und der Bach **258**

　Der Wanderer **124**

　Die Allmacht, op. 79, no. 2 **304**

　German Dance, op. 33,
　　no. 12 **167** ⊙ Track 24

　Im Abendroth (Posthumous) **102**

　Impromptu, op. 90,
　　no. 4, D. 899 **31** ⊙ Track 4

　Impromptu, op. 142,
　　no. 3 **175** ⊙ Track 28

　Ländler **23, 34** ⊙ Track 3

　Mass in A♭ major: Agnus Dei **322**

　Mass in E♭ major: Benedictus **196**;
　　Credo **267**

Schubert, Franz, *continued*
Mass in G major: Benedictus **303**;
Gloria **309**; Kyrie **283**
Quartet, D. 173 **210, 216**
Quartet in D major, D. 74 **94**
Quartet, op. 168, D. 112 **134, 274**
Quintet ("Die Forelle"),
op. 114, D. 667 **188**
Quintet, op. 163 **305**
Sonata, op. 42 **285** Track 69
Sonata, op. 53 **248**
Ständchen **136**
Symphony in C major ("The Great")
103, 194, 287
Symphony No. 8 ("Unfinished") **186,
293, 325**
Valses Nobles, op. 77 **24** Track 3
Valses Sentimentales, op. 50, no. 1,
D. 779 Track 9 **70**;
no. 18 **35** Track 5
Waltz **299** Track 74
Waltz, op. 9, no. 1, D. 365 **73** Track
9; no. 3 **51** Track 7; no. 14 **312**
Track 80
Wiegenlied, op. 98, no. 2 **18**
Schuman, William (1910–)
A Three-Score Set, II **432**
Schumann, Robert (1810–1856)
Album for the Young, op. 68:
Reiterstück **13**;
Soldatenmarsch **106**
Track 11
Arabeske, op. 18 **183**
Carnaval, op. 9: Arlequin **250**
Track 56;
Chiarina **144** Track 15
Dichterliebe, op. 48, no. 12: "Am
leuchtenden Sommermorgen" **290**
Faschingsschwank aus Wien, op. 26,
no. 3: Scherzino **27** Track 4
Genoveva, op. 81: Overture **333**
Kinderszenen, op. 15, no. 7: Träumerei
335 Track 88
Myrthen, op. 25, no. 24 **351**
Phantasiestücke, op. 12, no. 3: Warum?
354; no. 4, Grillen **101** Track 10
Sonata, op. 118ᵇ, Abendlied **236**;
Andante **180** Track 30;
Puppenwiegenlied **187**
Symphony No. 2, op. 61 **314**
Waldesgespräch, op. 39, no. 3 **330**
Widmung, op. 25, no. 1 **185**

Scriabin, Alexander (1872–1915)
Poem, op. 32, no. 2 **382** Track 96
Prelude, op. 13, no. 3 **319** Track 82
Shostakovitch, Dimitri (1906–1975)
Prelude, op. 34, no. 24 **380**
Sibelius, Jean (1865–1957)
Chanson Sans Paroles, op. 40, no. 2 **280**
Stockhausen, Karlheinz (1928–2007)
Klavierstücke, no. 2 **450**
Strauss, Johann (1825–1899)
Artist's Life Waltzes, op. 316, no. 3 **326**
Track 83
Die Fledermaus: Overture **320**
Strauss, Richard (1864–1949)
Der Rosenkavalier, Act I **281**; Act III **99**
Morgen, op. 27, no. 4 **357**
Stravinsky, Igor (1882–1971)
Five Fingers, Lento **397**
Petroushka, Danse Russe **406**;
Scene 2 **435**
Sonata for Two Pianos, II:
Theme with Variations **468**
The Rake's Progress: Prelude **434**
Sullivan, Sir Arthur (1842–1900)
H.M.S. Pinafore, "I'm Called Little
Buttercup" **84**

Tchaikovsky, Pyotr (1840–1893)
Mazurka **273** Track 65
Morning Prayer **205**
Track 36
Romeo and Juliet **298**
Song Without
Words **297** Track 73
Symphony No. 4, op. 36 **163**
Symphony No. 6, op. 74 **246**
The Witch **301** Track 76
Telemann, Georg Philipp (1681–1767)
Fantasie 1ᵉʳ Dozzina, no. 5 **155**
Fantasie No. 8 **114**
Teschner, Gustav Wilhelm
(1800–1883)
Schatz über alle Schätze **104**
Tessier, Charles (c. 1550–?)
Au joli bois je m'en vais **98**

Vaughan Williams, Ralph
(1872–1958)
London Symphony **411**
Verdi, Giuseppe (1813–1901)
Il Trovatore, Act II, no. 8 **261**; Act II,
no. 11 **126**

(Numbers in **bold** refer to *selection* numbers.)

La Traviata, Act I, no. 4 **119**; Act III: Prelude **286**

Rigoletto, Act I: Prelude **296**; no. 1 **91**; no. 2 **19**; no. 7 **30**; Act II: no. 7 **191**; no. 14 **56, 198**

Wagner, Richard (1813–1883)

Das Rheingold, Scene I, **152**

Der Engel **358**

Wotan's Farewell, Die Walküre, Act III, **345**

Lohengrin, Act I, scene 2 **344**

Prelude, Act I, Tristan and Isolde **363**

Rienzi: Overture **252**

Weber, Carl Maria von (1786–1826)

Euryanthe, op. 81: Overture **14, 341**

German Dance **16** Track 3

Oberon, Overture **22, 178**

Webern, Anton von (1883–1945)

Drei Lieder, op. 25, no. 1 **449**

Five Movements for String Quartet, op. 5, no. 4 **442**

Witt, Christian Friedrich (c. 1660–1716)

Passacaglia **171** Track 26

Index of Complete Pieces
(Including Examples of Small Forms)
(* denotes contrapuntal example)

Adderley,
Work Song **400**
Bach,
Cantata No. 4: Sinfonie* **366**
Chorale Prelude on "Christ lag in Todesbanden"* **368**
Chorale Prelude on "In dulci jubilo"* **367**
Christ lag in Todesbanden* **233**
Ein' Feste Burg is unser Gott* **348**
Es ist genug, so nimm, Herr* **349**
French Suite in C minor* **230**
In dulci jubilo* **232**
Invention No. 4, BWV 775* **371**
Invention No. 13, BWV 775* **372**
Sinfonia No. 3, BWV 789* **373**
The Well Tempered Clavier, Vol. I, Fugue 2* **374**
The Well Tempered Clavier, Vol. II, Fugue 9* **375**
Wachet auf ruft uns die Stimme* **231**
Bartók,
Fourteen Bagatelles, op. 6, no. 4 **398**
Fourteen Bagatelles, op. 6, no. 6 **419**
Little Pieces for Children, no. III **389**
Sketches, op. 9, no. 6 **418**
Beach,
Phantoms **361**
Beethoven,
Minuet in C **68**
Minuet **165**
Quartet, op. 18, no. 6 **349**
Scottish Dance **168**
Seiben Variationen über di Volkslied: "God Save the King" **359**
Seven Country Dances, no. 7 **33**
Sonata, op. 2, no. 3 (all movements) **365**
Sonata, op. 26, I **235**
Sonata, op. 109: III **277**
Sonatina in F major **239**
Theme from Six Easy Variations **328**
Berg,
Four Songs, op. 2, no. 3 **387**

Berger,
Two Episodes, I **445**
Brahms,
Chorale Prelude on "O wie selig seid ihr dich Frommer" * **369**
Liebeslieder Walzer, op. 52, no. 4 **256**
Waltz, op. 39 **237**
Casella,
Siciliana **399**
Chávez,
Ten Preludes, no. 1 **390**
Chopin,
Mazurka, op. Posth. 67, no. 2 **353**
Prelude, op. 28, no. 20 **263**
Prelude, op. 28, no. 6 **269**
Prelude, op. 28, no. 9 **347**
Crumb,
Madrigals, Book IV **453**
Debussy,
Pour le Piano: Sarabande **458**
Préludes, X: La Cathédrale engoutie **459**
Gershwin,
I Got Rhythm **241**
Porgy and Bess, "Summertime" **467**
Grieg,
Erotikon **355**
Norsk **172**
Handel,
Aria con Variazioni, Leçon No. 1, II **154**
Menuet* **234**
Prelude* **238**
Haydn,
Sonata in C♯ minor, Hob. XVI: 36, II **211**
Sonata in E minor, Hob. XVI: 34, III **218**
Sonata in G major, Hob. XVI: 27, Menuet **240**
Sonata in G major, Hob. XVI: 39, III **214**
Symphony No. 104, Hob. I: 104, II **254**
Hindemith,
Ludus Tonalis, Fuga undecima in B (Canon)* **463**
Piano Sonata no. 2: I **469**

Horne,
    Six Short Studies, Sixteenth Notes **456**
Joplin,
    A Breeze from Alabama: March and
        Two-Step **362**
Jordan,
    Jordu **388**
Kern,
    Can I Forget You? **206**
Krenek,
    Dancing Toys, op. 83, No. 1 **448**
Liszt,
    Il Pensieroso, from Années de
        Pèlerinage **356**
Macmillan,
    Piano Sonata, I **470**
Mendelssohn,
    Fugue No. 2, op. 35* **376**
    Lieder ohne Wörte, op. 30, No. 3 **352**
Milhaud,
    Saudades do Brazil, No. 6: Gavea **460**
Mozart,
    Minuet, K. 355 **350**
    Sonata, K. 282, Menuet I **215**
    Sonata, K. 309 (all movements) **364**
    Symphony No. 40, K. 550: III **360**
    Valse **25**
    Waltz, K. 567 **11**
Porter,
    Night and Day **466**
Prokofiev,
    Classical Symphony, op. 25: III **461**
    March from The Love of Three Oranges
        462
Purcell,
    Rigadoon* **169**
    Thy Hand Belinda, Dido and Aeneas*
        370
Rameau,
    Minuet **170**
Raksin,
    Laura **388**
Ravel,
    Sonatine, Mouvement II **457**

Rouse,
    Valentine **455**
Ruggles,
    Evocations, No. 1 **464**
Schönberg,
    Klavierstücke, op. 19, no.1 **440**
    Suite für Klavier, op. 25: Menuett **465**
Schubert,
    Dance **166**
    German Dance, op. 53, no. 12 **167**
    Ländler **34**
    Quartet, D. 175, II **216**
Schuman,
    A Three-Score Set, II **432**
Schumann,
    Kinderszenen, op. 15, no. 7: Träumerei
        335
    Myrthen, op. 25, no. 24 **351**
    Phantasiestücke, op. 12, no. 3: Warum?
        354
    Sonata, op. 118b, Abendlied **236**
Scriabin,
    Prelude, op. 13, no. 3 **319**
Strauss,
    Morgen, op. 27, no. 4 **357**
Stravinsky,
    Five Fingers: Lento **397**
    Sonata for Two Pianos, II: Theme with
        Variations **468**
    The Rake's Progress: Prelude **434**
Tchaikovsky,
    Morning Prayer **205**
Wagner,
    Der Engel **358**
    Prelude, Act I, Tristan and Isolde **363**
Webern,
    Drei Lieder, op. 25, no. 1 **449**
    Five Movements for String Quartet,
        op. 5, no. 4 **442**
Witt,
    Passacaglia* **171**

(Numbers in **bold** refer to *selection* numbers.)